'Out of control.' JOHN BOWLER, KALGOORLIE-BOULDER MAYOR

'Cheap shot.' GORDON BRADBERY, WOLLONGONG LORD MAYOR

'Bullying.' GEOFF BROCK MP, PORT PIRIE

'Not amusing, not entertaining, not fair and not close to the truth.' RON MCCULLOUGH, FORMER MOUNT ISA MAYOR

'Not funny at all, it's actually quite insulting. They're just trying to make a quick buck.' KON VATSKALIS, DARWIN LORD MAYOR

'I'm going to get Dutton to cancel this muppet's visa.' TONY PASIN MP, MOUNT GAMBIER

'Bugger off!' LEON STEPHENS, PORT PIRIE MAYOR

ON
SIDE ROAD
BITTER
PRIDE OF QUEENSLAND

SH*T TOWNS OF AUSTRALIA

THE GREAT AUSSIE ROAD TRIP

RICK FURPHY AND GEOFF RISSOLE

CONTENTS

INTRODUCTION

Aussies love a road trip. On the list of great Aussie traditions, roadies are right up there with barbies, sports that no other countries play, and medically dangerous levels of alcohol consumption. Packing up the ute and slogging for hours or days through an endless red sunburnt wasteland to get to some town that's only slightly less shit than where you came from is just part of living on the sprawling expanse of mediocrity known as Australia.

This book will guide you as you traverse Australia's shit towns—from Bondi to the bush, Blacktown to the black stump and back. The perfect companion to our previous volume, *Sh*t Towns of Australia*, *The Great Aussie Road Trip* covers dozens more crap towns and shitty city suburbs, as well as quintessential events, regional foods and other nuggets of knowledge to inform your turdy itinerary. For a personal touch, we've also included some of the fan mail we've received on our Facebook page, 'Shit Towns of Australia'—while the messages are real, the names have been changed.

This book presents seven epic road trips that together take in the most iconic shit towns in Anustralia. Each route links to the next (though you will need to catch a ferry from Melbourne or do some serious swimming to get to Tasmania). Bear in mind that there are numerous ways to get from Shit Town A to Shit Town B and endless possible shit town side trips, so depending on where you are, where you're going and what you want to see, use your preferred GPS device and your noggin to plot a route that suits.

Whether you're keen for a shit trip, a crap lap or a sewer tour, *The Great Aussie Road Trip* will help ensure you have a terrible time on your travels.

Key to symbols used in book

Drugs
Crime
Pollution

Bogans
Hippies
Wankers

Old people
Inbreds
Sex pests

Rednecks
Cannibals

Clockwise from top left: one of the Big Bulls at Rockhampton, Bundaberg's Big Rum Bottle, Sunshine Coast's Big Pineapple and Cairns' Big Nazi Captain Cook.

GREAT BOGAN ROAD

CAIRNS TO BRISBANE

CAIRNS
INNISFAIL
TOWNSVILLE
BOWEN
MACKAY
YEPPOON
ROCKHAMPTON
EMERALD
GLADSTONE

ROUTE NOTES

CAIRNS TO GLADSTONE

CAIRNS* See the bleached remains of the Great Barrier Reef!

INNISFAIL (page 14)

TOWNSVILLE* Car theft capital. Great place to get an insurance payout.

BOWEN (page 16)

MACKAY* Sugar and rednecks.

YEPPOON (page 17)

ROCKHAMPTON* Beef and rednecks.

OPTIONAL DETOUR: EMERALD (page 20)

GLADSTONE (page 21)

---

* Reviewed in *Sh*t Towns of Australia*

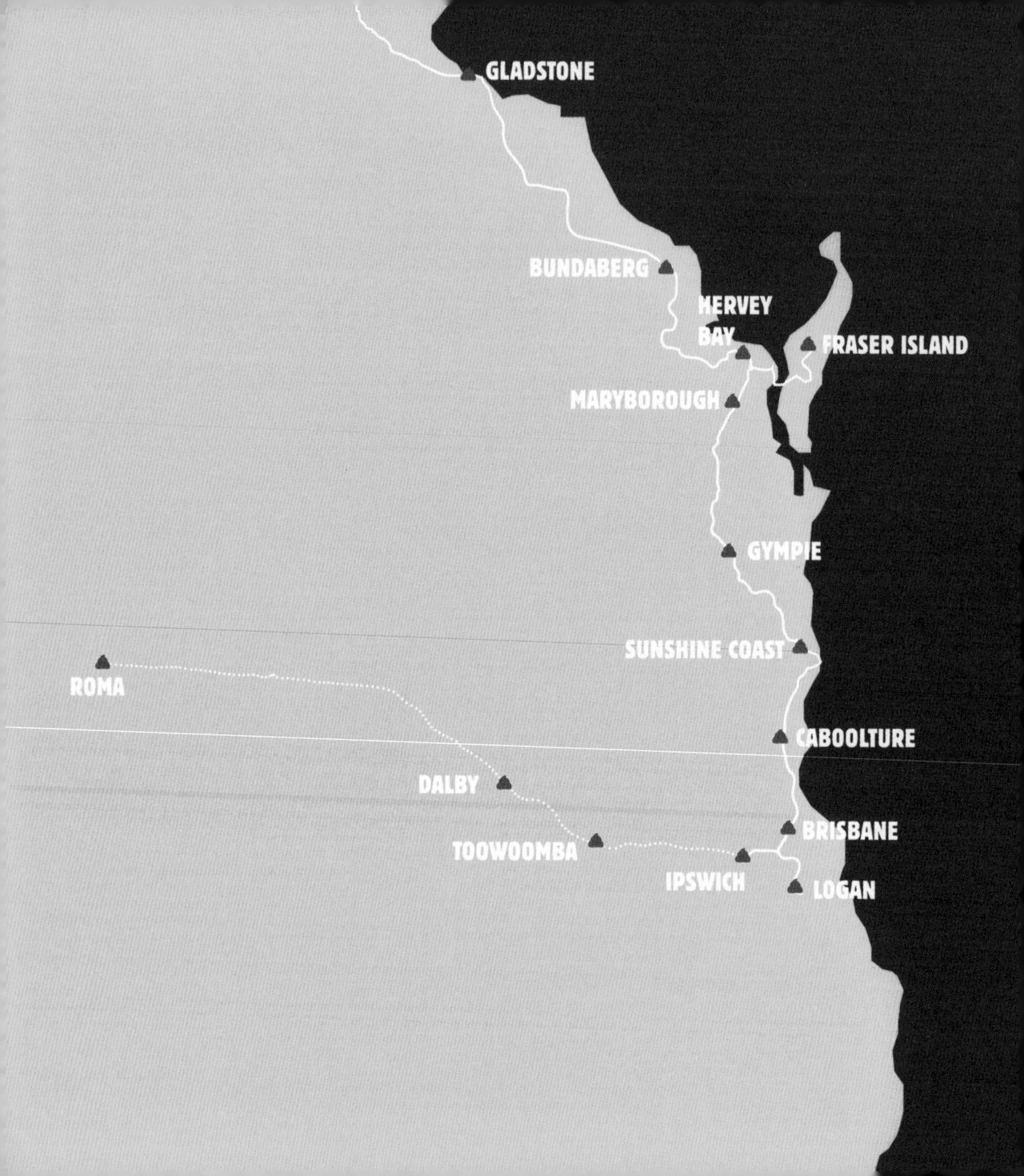

GLADSTONE

BUNDABERG

HERVEY BAY

FRASER ISLAND

MARYBOROUGH

GYMPIE

SUNSHINE COAST

ROMA

CABOOLTURE

DALBY

BRISBANE

TOOWOOMBA

IPSWICH

LOGAN

ROUTE NOTES

GLADSTONE TO LOGAN

BUNDABERG* Rum and rednecks.

HERVEY BAY (page 22)

FRASER ISLAND* Dingos and rednecks.

MARYBOROUGH (page 24)

GYMPIE (page 26)

SUNSHINE COAST* A slightly less awful version of the Gold Coast.

CABOOLTURE* More Logan than Logan.

BRISBANE* When it comes to culture, Brisbane is less Paris and more Parramatta (see Deception Bay, page 30, and Fortitude Valley, page 31).

IPSWICH* Brisbane's grotty basement (see Goodna, page 33).

OPTIONAL DETOURS: TOOWOOMBA* (Gardens and grey hair galore), **DALBY** (page 35) and **ROMA** (page 36).

LOGAN* There's a reason it rhymes with 'bogan'.

* Reviewed in *Sh*t Towns of Australia*

Innisfail

The centre of the Cassowary* Coast in the same way that an anus is the centre of an arse, Innisfail is best known for its sugar, bananas and cyclones. The perennial disaster zone is populated by a motley crew of inbred yokels, insurance fraudsters, slum lords, Italians, extortionate tradies and other assorted reprobates who are quite content with the town spending the majority of its time underwater.

Innisfail's constant rain and asphyxiating humidity mean it is inundated with mould, mosquitos and monsoons. The sweltering sweatbox is frequently flooded because some bright spark decided to build one of Australia's rainiest towns on the confluence of two rivers. Innisfail was seriously fucked up by Tropical Cyclone Larry in 2006, to which the local council responded in typical Queensland style by using relief funds to buy a $250,000 piano and putting the deputy mayor on the radio to request 'a truckload of piss so we can all get fucking drunk'.**

The first Europeans to happen upon the Innisfail area were victims of shipwreck, which remains the most popular reason for visiting. The town was originally named Geraldton but was renamed to avoid confusion with the Western Australian shithole of the same name. The new name was based on a traditional handle for Ireland that translates as 'Isle of Destiny', confusing because Innisfail is neither an island nor an Ireland, although most Queenslanders wish it was stranded somewhere in the North Atlantic. Innisfail marked this Irish link by naming its rugby league team the Leprechauns, a name about as intimidating as the Toowoomba Twinks or the Gladstone Grandmas.

Aside from cyclone season, the only other time Innisfail has entered the national consciousness was when shithouse seppo pop-rockers Sugar Ray filmed a music video at a local crocodile park in 2001. Sadly, the town failed to do the world a service and make sure Sugar Ray was eaten by a crocodile.

* A cassowary is an emu in drag.

** This is an actual thing that happened.

TOWN SLOGAN You Can't Spell Innisfail Without Fail!
ALSO KNOWN AS Innishole, Innisjail, Innisfailure, Epicfail, the Fail, Innardsfail, Incestfail, Penisfail, Anusfail.
MOST FAMOUS PERSON Rugby league legend Billy Slater, who appropriately looks like a leprechaun.

Bowen

Sensibly bypassed by the Bruce Highway and almost everyone on it, Bowen is best known for its Big Mango, a ten-metre-tall misshapen lump of fibreglass that looks more like a gangrenous gonad than a piece of fruit. The Big Mango was famously 'stolen' in 2014 in what was later revealed to be a publicity stunt for a fast-food chain. Keen-eyed observers were suspicious of the 'theft' from the outset as clearly no one would want to steal that piece of shit.

Bowen is also notable as one of the filming locations for the Baz Luhrmann atrocity *Australia*, and the site of the equally cringeworthy 'Bowenwood' signage that adorned a local water tower for a full decade following the film's release. Bowen stood in for Darwin in the film, a good choice as both places are shitholes. Frankly, any town capable of doubling for Darwin in the 1940s deserves to be bombed by the Japanese. Aside from the Big Mango and the big boring water tower, visitors to Bowen can also peruse a series of 27 murals depicting typical activities in the region, such as cane farming, mining and smoking meth.

Bowen is also home to the Abbot Point coal terminal, which is ideally located thanks to the area's deep water close to shore, its relative proximity to coalfields, and a natural garbage tip off the coast called the Great Barrier Reef, which is apparently the perfect place to dump dredging spoil. Abbot Point is used for exporting millions of tonnes of coal each year to overseas global-warming factories, which is great news for people who get a boner for bushfires.

TOWN SLOGAN Top of the Shitsunday.
ALSO KNOWN AS Bowentown, Bowenwood, Blowin' Bowen, Bogen, Bowel, Tropical Lithgow.
DID YOU KNOW? Bowen's combination of oppressive heat, relentless wind and interminable boredom renders many residents with a short fuse, a phenomenon known as Irritable Bowen Syndrome.

Yeppoon

Yeppoon couldn't decide whether it wanted to be a sleepy seaside village or a bustling tourist mecca so it did neither, resulting in a big fat nothing. The town is completely devoid of jobs so its few employed residents are forced to commute 40 minutes to Rockhampton, making it ideal for people who made a sea change so they could enjoy the mind-numbing boredom of living in a comatose coastal carbuncle as well as the soul-destroying tedium of driving to another town every day to a job they hate. The town is also overrun with silver-haired septuagenarians biding their time until someone lowers a pillow over their face while the waves lap gently on the shore. Anyone who willingly lives in a second-rate Rockhampton has clearly given up on life.

The Big Butthole, Yeppoon.

Nightlife in Yeppoon consists of getting some Yeppoontang at the Strand Hotel, passing out on the Keppel Kraken or pouring your pension into the pokies at the sailing club. The town's most popular feature is the Yeppoon Lagoon, up there with such other famous rhyming tourist attractions as the Bangkok Wok and the Innisfail Gaol. Another attraction is Shell World, housing 20,000 shells, which might prove fascinating if you are an old, old lady. Yeppoon is also home to an abandoned Japanese tourist resort that was welcomed to town in the 1980s in true redneck fashion: with a bombing by xenophobic locals. The town's beaches are covered with glass and rubbish and the council is unwilling to install bins because they would get stolen. There is no affordable accommodation for backpackers, which is okay because no one under 80 wants to go there anyway. All things considered, the Yeppoonese have done an impressive job of turning a spectacular natural location into an all-round awful place.

TOWN SLOGAN Wet or Dry, The Poon is Always Open For Business!
ALSO KNOWN AS The Poon, Yeppoo, Yeppoontang, Yeppoonani.

I'm victorian born been here since I was 16 I'm now 44 iv seen some shit in my time here ,its my home so if u got nothing nice 2 say dont say anything no 1 wnts 2 hear your shit so go eat a dick and piss off back 2 wot ever shit ton u leaked out of **(Dwaynis Fivehead, Mackay)**

So many gelous people, it's discussing and iffensive **(Jennaveen Gronkford, Emerald)**

WHAT a miss informed fake news Fukwit!!! Your lies scare our children, you are child abusers. We are sick of your crap and revenge will come. **(Staniel Lump, Gladstone)**

Emerald

Emerald earned its name from its early reliance on mining gemstones but its main industry is now coalmining, so a more appropriate moniker might be 'Coalville', 'Soottown' or 'Main Reason the Entire Planet is Going to Die a Fiery Death City'. Instead, all the towns in the area are named like bogans' daughters: Emerald, Sapphire, Anakie, Shazza. Emerald also produces large volumes of cotton to send to Bangladesh for child slaves to make into T-shirts to send back to Australia. In other words, the town's economy relies on miners and minors.

Emerald's most prominent attraction is a giant version of a Van Gogh painting perched on an oversized easel, a tribute to the town's long history of self-harm. Another item of interest is a piece of fossilised wood outside the town hall estimated to be 250 million years old, making it slightly younger than the majority of Emerald's residents. Local waterhole Lake Maraboon is famously three times larger than Sydney Harbour and ten times as shit. Popular among water sport enthusiasts and anglers, Maraboon is a great place to get impaled on a hook or have

Easel-y one of Australia's worst tourist attractions.

a large man piss in your face. As the 'Gateway to the Outback', Emerald is also a convenient place to bury any dead backpackers you might have rattling around in your car boot.

Gladstone ☢✌

Gladstone's main claim to fame is its position on the edge of the bleached carcass of the Great Barrier Reef, which is what happens when you plonk a gargantuan coal terminal, an alumina refinery, an aluminium smelter and three LNG plants in a World Heritage area, then dredge the fuck out of the seabed and dump the sludge all over the coral. Replete with the ubiquitous stench of caustics and an eerie green sky, the reef-wrecking seaside shitnest of Gladstone exploits its location to lure in tourists, who apparently enjoy swimming with dead dugongs at coaldust-coated beaches in the shadow of hulking industrial monstrosities and emerging from the polluted sea covered in mysterious sores.

Gladstone is primarily inhabited by self-righteous bogan mercenaries who not only think it's okay to destroy a natural wonder of the world so they can buy an HSV but also that Australia owes them a debt of gratitude for doing so. The only upside of Gladstone's environmental vandalism is that the toxic air quickly strips the shiny red paint off these brand-new boganmobiles' bonnets.

Originally called Port Curtis, the city was renamed Gladstone because you're only glad to be there if you're stoned. The poo pit was once promoted as a possible capital of Queensland, but even then it was so shit that the powers that be preferred the burgeoning boganopolis of Brisbane. In 1945, the crew of a US Air Force plane were so disturbed by the sight of Gladstone that they flew headfirst into the ground. These days, the city is conveniently home to a cyanide plant, which should prove useful if the locals ever realise what a disgrace their town is and decide to make a quick exit.

ALSO KNOWN AS Gladdy, Happy Rock, Happy Knackers, Gladhole, Sadstone, Sadrock, Gladstoned, Crapstone, Gallstone, Globstain, Mount Isa by the Sea.
MOST FAMOUS PEOPLE Rugby league player and part-time cartoonist Gary Larson, country singer Hayley Marston and circus trash James Henry Ashton.
DID YOU KNOW? Many locals suffer from a condition known as 'Glad eye', a weeping infection caused by prolonged exposure to airborne contaminants.

Hervey Bay

Sprawled along the shores of an unsightly silty mudflat, Hervey Bay is a tangled clump of villages stuck together by endless caravan parks and old

people asylums—a fatberg of shit towns. Pervy Bay's most popular activities are visiting Fraser Island to get eaten by a dingo and whale watching, which consists of cruising up the coast to gawp at people from Rockhampton.

Hervey Bay's lack of normal entertainment options makes it ideal for retirees seeking 'peace and quiet' so they can simulate the conditions of their impending death away from the disruptive gaze of immigrants and gays. The majority of the town's elderly inmates are actually refugees from Victoria searching for somewhere that resembles the Australia they grew up in (i.e. white and dull as shit). The place is so stacked with snooty boomers that it holds the world record for the longest parade of electric mobility scooters, which is apparently the sort of thing that passes for fun in Scurvy Bay.

Hervey Bay claims to be the 'Caravan Capital of Australia', which is a bit like boasting about having the most venereal diseases in your cell block. Herpes Bay's countless caravan parks are home to an array of feral residents who enjoy a spot of everything from hitting each other with hammers to biting policemen after 'riding the glass-bottom boat'. These JobSeeker tweakers actually have much in common with their elderly neighbours: they don't work, they're covered in scabs and missing their teeth, and one day soon they won't wake up. It's a sweet release most people in Hervey Hole can only hope for.

TOWN SLOGAN Home of the Newlyweds, Nearly-Deads and Meth Heads.
ALSO KNOWN AS Hervey Hole, Scurvy Bay, Pervy Bay, Herpes Bay, Shardy Bay.
DID YOU KNOW? Hervey Bay is pronounced 'Harvey Bay' as a tribute to filmmaker Harvey Weinstein.

Maryborough

Not to be confused with its Victorian shit town namesake, the Queensland craphole of Maryborough is best known as the birthplace of *Mary Poppins* author P.L. Travers, who left when she was a small child and never returned because it was shit. Travers' famously psychedelic book and subsequent film adaptations about a magical flying nanny were inspired by the author's memories of her many drug-addled hallucinations as a toddler in the town. In fact, the book was originally called *Fear and Loathing on the Fraser Coast*. Mary Poppins even takes her first

name from the town, while her last name is an unsubtle allusion to heroin poppies. Fun fact: the Mary Poppins song 'A Spoonful of Sugar' is actually about cocaine, 'Stay Awake' is about meth and 'Feed the Birds' is about public masturbation.

Mary Poppins is honoured with a statue and even themed traffic lights in Maryborough, the town's way of acknowledging its sizeable population of opioid addicts. The preponderance of local violent criminals is celebrated in a similar way, with a giant shotgun-toting Ned Kelly looming over a servo, presumably with the intent of robbing it for a carton of durries.

The highlight of Maryborough's social calendar is the annual Mary Poppins Festival, which is probably why the place is commonly known as 'Maryboring'. Other popular nicknames include 'Scaryborough' and 'Marry-Ya-Brother', both of which are eerily appropriate for the pest-infested incest-fest of a joint. Locals prefer the label the 'Heritage City of Queensland', an odd marketing angle when your history consists of a bunch of Indigenous massacres, enslavement of South Sea islanders and Australia's only outbreak of pneumonic plague. The heritage slogan is at least accurate in the sense that the town is full of old things —old buildings, old attitudes and old people.

TOWN SLOGAN Hervey Bay's Toilet.
ALSO KNOWN AS Marbra, Mrbr, the Burrow, Maryhole, Maryboring, Scaryborough, Terrorborough, Methyborough, Marybugger, Marry-Ya-Brother.
DID YOU KNOW? Maryborough was named after Mary Borough, a colonial prostitute who serviced local whalers.

Gympie

Originally named Nashville due to all the incest, Gympie took its current name not from BDSM enthusiasts or cripples, as one might assume, but from the world's most horrible plant. The gympie is a stinging tree covered in toxic needles, also known as the stinging brush or the suicide plant. Legend has it that an Australian World War II soldier shot himself after inadvertently using a gympie leaf as toilet paper. Like its botanic namesake, the town of Gympie is also

dangerous, covered in needles and smeared with faeces.

The Queensland craphole owes its existence to the discovery of gold in the local area, which saw the town swiftly filled with the sort of reprobates who would travel the world to stand in bollocks-deep water trying to find a shiny nugget just so they wouldn't have to find a real job. The gold rush also marked the only time in history that anyone has ever been excited to visit Gympie. Consequently, Gympie is known as 'the town that saved Queensland', so we have them to thank for maroon-clad morons pissed up on XXXX king-hitting strangers while yelling 'Queenslander!'

Like most places in Australia

not sophisticated enough for a heroin problem, Gympie is a deadset mecca for meth. In fact, it's a little-known fact that the town's name is an acronym for 'Grab Ya Meth Pipe, Ice Everywhere!' Gympanzees are also famously partial to a bit of cannabis, hooning, burglary, racism and putting people through woodchippers. The town's reputation for crime is so widespread that it has become known as 'Helltown' (though in true Gympie style, this term was coined by a convicted paedophile writing in a porno mag).

Gymphole has a range of visitor attractions, all of which are shit. The Mary Valley Rattler is an inefficient old tourist train that gives a great view of rubbish tips and car wreckers' yards and is also the name of a violent lovemaking manoeuvre. The Gympie Pyramid is a terraced hill touted by the intellectually challenged as evidence of ancient Egyptian/Aztec/alien colonisation and is also the name of a violent lovemaking manoeuvre. The Big Pineapple was demolished in 2008 when authorities realised that no one in Gympie eats fruit and was replaced by Australia's only giant revolving KFC bucket. Enjoying a trip to Gympie is about as likely as Pauline Hanson opening a kebab shop.

TOWN SLOGAN Bring Out the Gympie!
ALSO KNOWN AS Gimpy, Helltown, Gymphole, The Hole, Gymptanamo Bay.
DID YOU KNOW? In 2013 two teens tried to steal the Mary Valley Rattler but were thwarted by not knowing how to drive a train.

Who ever wrote this has a big fat cock growing off his forehead **(Billy-Bob Doorknob, Gladstone)**

It's a great town went to a wedding there great piss up.. Punch up at wedding and I got to root one of my new in-laws **(Mick Piston, Gladstone)**

Wow. What a derogative post. Guess the author is educated **(Merveen Plank, Bundaberg)**

Deception Bay

Wedged between Brisbane and the Sunshine Coast and shunned by both, the municipality of Moreton Bay is a cluster of some of Australia's shittiest suburbs, including Caboolture, Morayfield and Strathpine, making it Bogan Voltron. Among its worst components is Deception Bay.

Deception Bay is so named because early British settlers were deceived into thinking it was a place worth living in. Incidentally, 'deception' also happens to be a portmanteau of the suburb's two principal pastimes: depression and conception. Populated by a clot of gronks who were pushed out of Brisbane by rising living costs and increased police presence, Depression Bay is a sloppy shit of a suburb that spoils some prime seaside real estate (if you can describe an endless stretch of mud as 'prime'). Along with Logan and Ipswich to the south, Conception Bay and its mongrel Moreton neighbours ensure that Queensland's capital is encircled by a metaphorical moat of shit. The suburb regularly makes the news for criminal activity, continually surprising Brisbanites who are usually blissfully unaware that anything exists north of Brighton.

Local attractions in the Deception Bay area include shipwrecks, car wrecks and plenty of pubs with cement floors for hosing the blood off. There are numerous entertainment options, such as setting off a homemade bomb at a sportsground, spray painting a cock and balls on someone's car, or getting in a fight at a shopping mall. Or you could go for a scenic stroll through the decaying housing estates and get beaten up for your shoes. D-Bay's greatest asset of all is its good sealed roads and easy access to the Bruce Highway, ideal for driving away and never coming back.

ALSO KNOWN AS D-Bay, Dog Bay, Depression Bay, Conception Bay, Decrepit Bay, Deficient Bay, Derelict Bay.

MOST FAMOUS PERSON The Moreton Bay region is responsible for inflicting mass amounts of aural punishment on the world by shitting out both Keith Urban and the Bee Gees.

DID YOU KNOW? Every summer Deception Bay is inundated by screaming diseased bats due to the annual bushfires in the Sunshine Coast hinterland.

Fortitude Valley

Fortitude Valley is considered Brisbane's entertainment capital but would be more accurately described as a post-coital queef reincarnated as a suburb. Jammed full of dodgy nightclubs, dive bars, pokie dens, brothels, strip clubs, sex shops and Asian takeaways, the suburb is a sleazy Shangri-la for Brisbane bogans who can't be fucked flying to Pattaya. Ironically, despite all the happy pills, happy hours and happy endings, Fortitude Valley is actually a miserable hole.

The area's first European settlers were Scottish immigrants who were tricked into moving there by the promise of free land and ten-dollar hand jobs. Immediately filled with regret, they named it Fortitude Valley because you need copious reserves of fortitude to live there. The suburb was such a cesspit of sin that in the 1920s the Catholic Church decided it was in dire need of a giant cathedral. However, even the Southern Hemisphere's biggest church couldn't stem the flow of filth in Fortitude Valley, and the project was abandoned in despair after four decades of construction. The site now houses a six-storey sex complex called Satan's Sluts.

No one actually lives in Fortitude Valley, but each night the sordid suburb is filled with shitloads of pill-popping roid ragers in skin-tight Tapout shirts power-chundering on shop windows, running in front of cars and coward-punching each other for shits and giggles, sweaty sex pests crawling the streets while their wives and kids sleep at home, and gaggles of eighteen-year-old girls wearing almost nothing seeing how long they can dance, squeal and take pouty selfies before their drinks get spiked. By day, the streets are covered in mentally disturbed individuals screaming screeds of nonsense while sitting in puddles of their own piss.

Several attempts have been made to change the Valley's image as a den of debauchery but have met strong resistance. In fact, the suburb is Australia's first official 'Special Entertainment Precinct', meaning its nocturnal carnage is protected by the government, making it the exact opposite of Sydney.

ALSO KNOWN AS The Valley, The Vag, Prostitute Valley.

Goodna

This review has been stolen.

TOWN SLOGAN Good? Nah!
ALSO KNOWN AS G Town, G Block, the 43rd District, Badna, Hoodna, Nogoodna.
FUN FACT Goodna residents looted evacuated homes during both the 1974 and 2011 floods.
MOST FAMOUS PERSON Full-time homophobic social media troll and part-time rugby player Israel Folau, who even has a street named after him in Goodna. The street sign was stolen three times before it was unveiled by former mayor Paul Pisasale, who's currently serving a seven-year prison sentence on a range of unrelated charges.
DID YOU KNOW? Goodna's name is derived from the Indigenous word 'goona', meaning 'shit'.

Bundaberg is the number one manufacturer of garbage trucks in Australia. You snob-faced FUCKARSES! **(Steevin Weenis, Bundaberg)**

your whole page is a bunch of shit you would not no shit if you wiped it of your own ass . gutless in breads **(Wal Wingnut, Hervey Bay)**

Be weary of calmer, you never know what lays ahead. **(Sheralyn Offal, Hervey Bay)**

Dalby

Most regional towns spruik themselves with the old cliché 'where city meets country'. Dalby is more 'where country meets country' (or more accurately, 'where incest meets boredom'). The town has a rich rural diversity, which means it stinks of at least four different types of animal shit. Dalby is so dull it makes the nearby retirement home of Toowoomba look like Surfers Paradise during schoolies (only with more pill-popping and even more orgies). Dalbatians' main activities are growing grain to convert into alcohol and consuming the fruits of their labour in copious quantities to numb the existential horror of living in Dalby.

Dalby was largely settled by migrants from the Isle of Man in the mid-nineteenth century. However, the population didn't really take off until migrants started arriving from the Isle of Woman. The town found a purpose in the early 1900s when it was used by the state government as a gulag for tuberculosis patients. In 1904, the council opened therapeutic thermal baths using artesian water from a local bore, which then closed in 1938 when people decided it was better to treat their ailments with medicine rather than by sitting in tepid water with a bunch of disease-addled Dalbetics (this modern twentieth-century wisdom is yet to reach New South Wales' Northern Rivers).

Most towns have war memorials or statues of their founders. Dalby has a monument to the South American cactus moth, expressing the town's gratitude to the insect for wiping out a plant they didn't like. The 'Mothument' is one of two places in Dalby listed as tourist attractions on Wikipedia, along with the local cemetery. The best attraction is actually the road out of there, but being largely one lane and riddled with potholes, that's also shit.

ALSO KNOWN AS Doleby, Smellby, Hellby, Foulby, Shitby.
MOST FAMOUS PERSON Margot Robbie, the only attractive person ever born in Dalby.

Roma

They say that Rome wasn't built in a day, but apparently Roma was. The Queensland crapper was clearly named after the Italian capital because it resembles a city that's just been sacked by barbarians. Australia's 'Infernal City' is inhabited largely by drug addicts (Queensland's Romans prefer a glass barbie to a pizza oven), sexual deviants (fiddling with themselves while Roma burns) and grey-haired bogans driving around their fourteen-year-old girlfriends (when it comes to romance, Roma is less *Romeo and Juliet* and more Roman Polanski). When in Roma don't do as the Romans do, or you'll most likely wake up naked in a police cell with a long list of charges and a couple of new STDs.

Appropriately rhyming with such delightful words as coma, stoma and melanoma, Roma has been in the fast lane to oblivion since local coal seam gas projects ended. The town is now surrounded by fields full of idle earthmoving machines and littered with empty hotels and an airport that no one uses. Roma

Roma's famous chode tree.

also features exorbitant rental prices despite being six hours from the ocean—the only time it has waterfront property is when the entire town floods every year. It's no wonder that Roma was referred to by early settlers as 'The Bungil'—or in other words, 'The Fuck-Up'.

They say that all roads lead to Roma. Fortunately, that also means that all roads lead out again. Take one.

ALSO KNOWN AS Coma, Stoma, The Eternal Shitty.
MOST FAMOUS PERSON Darren Lockyer, gravelly-voiced hair plug recipient and NRL legend.

EVENT
AUSTRALIA DAY (26 JANUARY)

If Bathurst (page 82) is Bogan Christmas then Australia Day is Redneck Mardi Gras, the perfect excuse for hordes of gronks to imbibe enough alcohol to paralyse an elephant, discard their shirts, and drape themselves in their best Chinese-made Aussie flags to match the Southern Cross tattoos that they got in Bali. It's the one day of the year when the whole country becomes Cronulla.

Australia is the only country that celebrates the day it was invaded as its national holiday, which is a bit like America hosting a Pearl Harbor Day pool party or France hosting any number of events for any number of invasions. Apparently, the most appropriate way to commemorate nicking an entire continent off its rightful

owners is by ingesting copious amounts of badly barbecued meat and cheap piss before chundering it up again all over the stolen ground.

While particularly beloved by bogans, Australia Day is truly a day for all Australians: bogans get to be a bit racist, and wowsers with arts degrees get something to whinge about on Twitter before showing off their 'wokeness' by performing a Welcome to Country at their vegan barbecue in order to root a white girl with dreadlocks and hairy legs. Everybody wins!

If you're in a major city, round out the day by watching a spectacular display of fireworks that will terrorise the native wildlife and quite possibly start a catastrophic bushfire. Aussie Aussie Aussie!

Coffs locals are clearly compensating for something (hint: small penises).

CRACKPOT COAST

BRISBANE TO SYDNEY

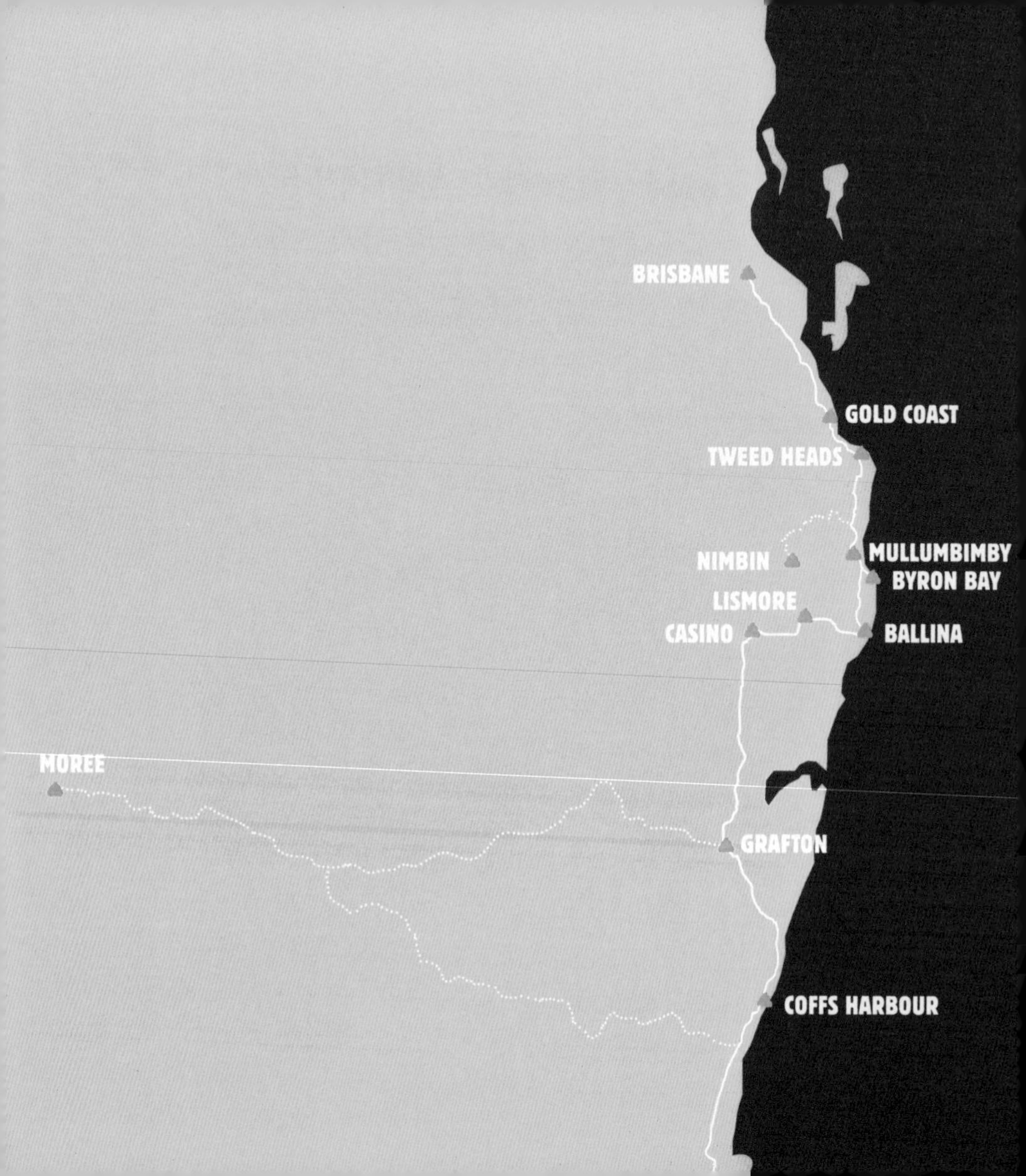

BRISBANE

GOLD COAST

TWEED HEADS

MULLUMBIMBY

NIMBIN

BYRON BAY

LISMORE

CASINO

BALLINA

MOREE

GRAFTON

COFFS HARBOUR

ROUTE NOTES

BRISBANE TO COFFS HARBOUR

GOLD COAST* Australia's version of Las Vegas, i.e. a tacky tourist trap with a shit casino and an unending parade of timeshare presentations.

TWEED HEADS (page 46)

OPTIONAL DETOUR: NIMBIN* Basically a town-sized supermarket for drugs.

MULLUMBIMBY (page 47)

BYRON BAY* The Gold Coast for people who prefer their Meter Maids to have hairy pits.

BALLINA (page 50)

LISMORE* A subtropical shitter built in a big hole.

CASINO* Beef and hillbillies.

GRAFTON* Try to make it across the infamous bendy bridge alive.

OPTIONAL DETOUR: MOREE (page 51)

COFFS HARBOUR* Big Banana.

* Reviewed in *Sh*t Towns of Australia*

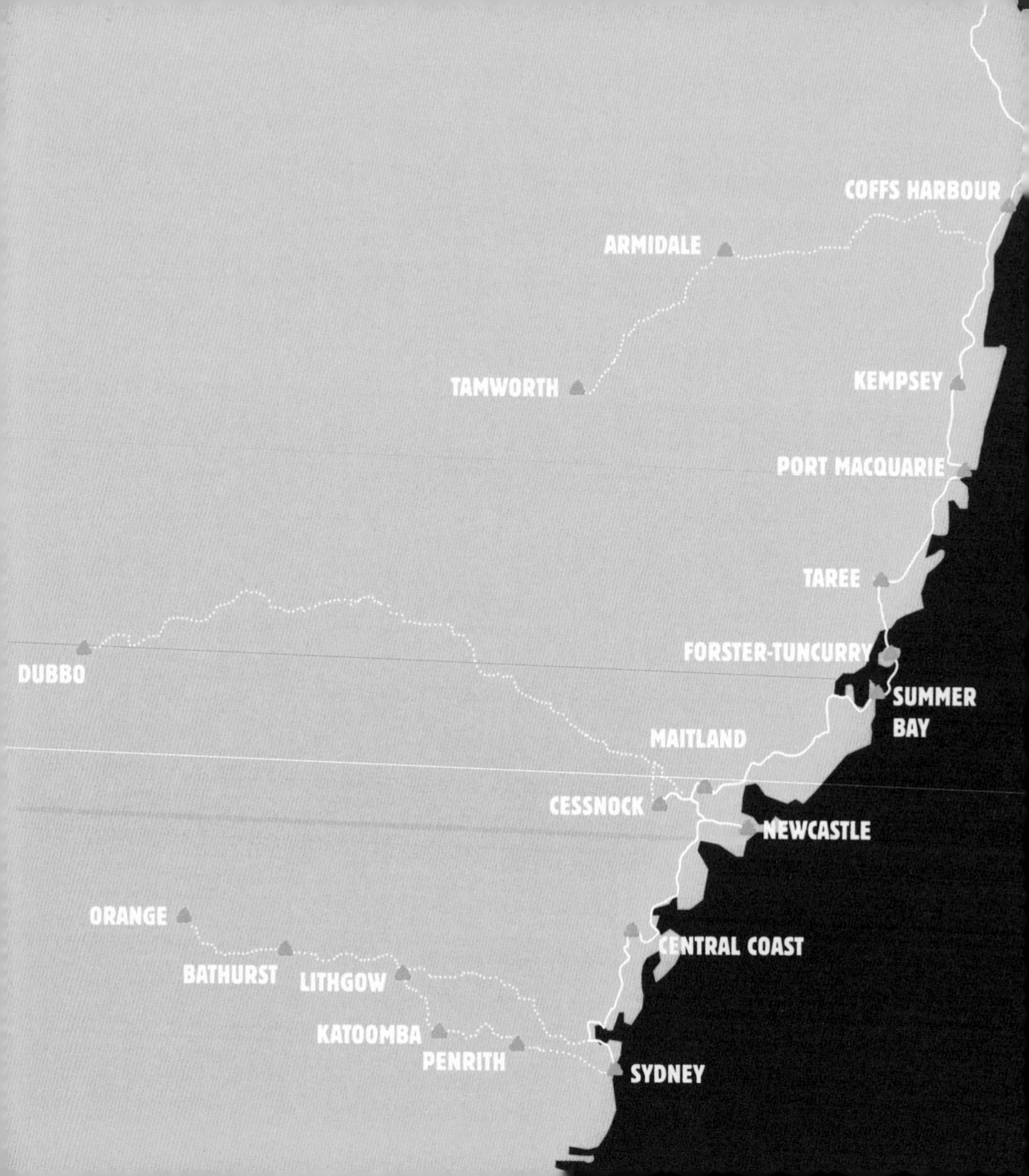

COFFS HARBOUR
ARMIDALE
TAMWORTH
KEMPSEY
PORT MACQUARIE
TAREE
FORSTER-TUNCURRY
DUBBO
SUMMER BAY
MAITLAND
CESSNOCK
NEWCASTLE
ORANGE
CENTRAL COAST
BATHURST
LITHGOW
KATOOMBA
PENRITH
SYDNEY

ROUTE NOTES

COFFS HARBOUR TO SYDNEY

OPTIONAL DETOUR: ARMIDALE* and **TAMWORTH*** (country music and incest).

KEMPSEY (page 54)

PORT MACQUARIE* Overrun with two of Australia's biggest pests: koalas and old people.

TAREE (page 55)

FORSTER-TUNCURRY (page 56)

SUMMER BAY (page 58)

MAITLAND (page 60)

OPTIONAL DETOUR: DUBBO* Great place to get stabbed by a five-year-old.

CESSNOCK (page 63)

NEWCASTLE* The rusted carcass of a port with a decrepit CBD welded on.

CENTRAL COAST* Mount Druitt by the sea (see Woy Woy, page 65).

OPTIONAL DETOUR: LITHGOW* to **BATHURST*** (home of the Bathurst 1000, a.k.a. Bogan Christmas; page 82) and **ORANGE*** (famous for apples). Return via **KATOOMBA** (page 68) and **PENRITH***.

SYDNEY* A bunch of shit towns loosely amalgamated into an overcrowded, overpriced and overrated shitropolis (pages 69–81).

* Reviewed in *Sh*t Towns of Australia*

Tweed Heads

Smeared either side of the New South Wales–Queensland border, Tweed Heads is Coolangatta's malformed and malevolent conjoined twin. The 'Home Brand Gold Coast' originally emerged as a place for Queensland's thrifty reprobates to take advantage of New South Wales' liberal gambling and prostitution laws while travelling the shortest possible distance. To this day, the border town is packed with pokie dens and brimming with brothels. Due to Queensland's stubborn shunning of daylight saving, during summer Tweed Heads becomes a ratchet time machine where you can travel in time simply by crossing a street. Unfortunately, it doesn't transport you to a time when Tweed Heads isn't a shithole.

There are two types of people who live in Tweed Heads: juvenile gangsters turning the place into Eshay Disneyland and retirees looking for somewhere by the sea to run out the clock. The entire generation between is mysteriously missing. The town takes its name from its proliferation of grumpy grandads, the only people who would be seen dead wearing tweed (and soon they will be). In fact, Tweed Heads has the largest tweedophile population in all of Australia. Unfortunately, the ample geriatrics are sitting ducks for the roid-raging failed league players and psychotic trust-fund pinga rats who make up the rest of the local population. Packs of delinquents roam Tweed's wide riverside streets with impunity, stabbing or coward-punching random residents and smearing poo on people's property for literal shits and giggles.

A popular daytrip from Tweed Heads is the lush Lamington National Park, replete with coconut, sponge and chocolate trees. The town itself also features a number of parks, though the council recently resorted to tearing the roof and walls off one popular picnic area because there was too much George Michaeling going on. Considering Tweed Heads is essentially Australia's Tijuana—a crime-riddled border-straddling abortion—it's appropriate that it sits in the long shadow of the ominously named Mount Warning; other local landmarks include Point Danger, Beware Hill and You're Going To Die Bay.

ALSO KNOWN AS Weed Heads, Twit Heads, Tweed Hoods, Two Heads, Tijuana Heads.

Mullumbimby

Nestled in the arse-backwards Northern Rivers region, Mullumbimby is an escape from the social decorum and modern conveniences of the First World. It's known for its 'hippie ethos', a simple and deluded way of life that's essentially an elaborate ploy for blokes with male pattern baldness to root confused women in their early twenties. The town is infested by all manner of deodorant dodgers, from dole-bludging 'artists' to preachy vegans and hairy nudists, as well as increasing numbers of sea changing C-list celebrities and trustafarian big-city rejects priced out of Byron Bay, desperately trying to live a 'hippie lifestyle' by opening pretentious cafes and dangling some beads from the rear-view mirrors of their $140K Land Rovers.

Mullumbimby is the ideal place to do some tantric yoga while writing a snarky tweet about how microwave popcorn causes schizophrenia, try to cure your venereal disease with reiki, or sample some local artisanal methamphetamine. In fact, you can get just about anything there (except a steak, a shower, a useful education or a flu shot). A popular local attraction is the Crystal Castle, which despite its name is not a meth lab but actually a hippie wonderland where you can get your chakras realigned if you accidentally used 5G to download your latest conspiracy video.

Mullumbimby's major industry is euphemistically called 'alternative health' or 'wellness', which is ironic because the town's health stats are nothing to trumpet, with life expectancy, child mortality and rates of all cancers worse than the national averages. In fact, Mullumbimby's diseases are so advanced that it already has COVID-22. It's no coincidence that Measlebimby is also the anti-vaxxer capital of Australia, with the average level of scientific literacy lying somewhere between Donald Trump and Paleo Pete. Most residents are terrified of immunisations but would happily fill their bodies with frog poison if their shaman told them to. Nevertheless, the same Mullumbimbos were no doubt first to put their hands up for a coronavirus vaccination when their magic vibration machines and herbal butt plugs inexplicably failed to do the job.

TOWN SLOGAN The Biggest Little Hole in Australia.
ALSO KNOWN AS Mullum, Bimby, Measlebimby, Methambimby.

Horrible, nasty, fascist overtones—the enemy! Nimbin rocks, if you mock Nimbin you're a moron and the natural enemy of real human beings everywhere. (Moonpetal Pondscum, Nimbin)

You're fb page is putrid . Some body has a damaged soul. Maby some body has been run out of towns his whole line. Honestly. Shit . Move out of AUSTRALIA (Maryleigh Frogtits, Mullumbimby)

Funny how just when we stand up for our rights, eg five G. Morons like the person (or government stooge), post crap like this, crawl back to the cold and bitter place you come from stooge, (Tim Foilhat, Mullumbimby)

Story written by a inner city cafe latte sipping butt ugly Vegan wanka who can't get a root . (Brian Niplips, Casino)

MOST FAMOUS PERSON As well as the re-emergence of preventable diseases, Mullumbimby is also responsible for another of the world's biggest contemporary disasters, Iggy Azalea. Meanwhile, Mullumbimby blow-ins include conspiracy theorist Paleo Pete and celebrity hippie Russell Brand.

DID YOU KNOW? In addition to pot and pockmarks, Mullumbimby is also known for its potholes.

Ballina ☮ 🥸 ⌐

Ballina boasts that it's the gateway to Byron Bay—or in other words, an ideal spot to pick up some bongos and measles en route to a dirty hippie fuck-fest disguised as a surf camp, yoga retreat or cult meeting. The Northern Rivers shitter is the site of the Ballina Byron Gateway Airport—the 'Byron Gateway' bit was added to the name in 2005 in a bid to trick more people into visiting Ballina. Unfortunately for Ballina, it only encouraged throngs of tourists to fly into the airport before fucking off to Byron as quickly as possible. Fortunately for Ballina, most of the people flying in and fucking off are pseudo-hippie boofheads and aspiring social media influencers anyway.

In contrast to the OnlyFans content creators passing through, Ballina's resident population has an average age of about 100, thanks to old people's irresistible attraction to sand. Local activities include losing your teeth at the beach, getting into a road-rage incident on your mobility scooter, and having a heart attack while yelling at some youths.

Ballina's premier landmark is

the Big Prawn, one of Australia's most butt-ugly Big Things. There's a good reason why prawns are small: so people don't have to be confronted by their creepy features at full size—until now. Plonked unceremoniously in the car park of Ballina Bunnings, the gargantuan fibreglass and concrete crustacean is enough to put any home handyman off their Sunday sausage sizzle.

Moree

Clogging up the junction of the Newell and Grindr highways, Moree is a notoriously remote rat hole located a good chunk of a day's drive from both Sydney and

Brisbane. Residents of both cities would probably agree that the distance isn't quite far enough.

Famous as New South Wales' crime capital, Moree is packed with marauding mobs of morons burning cars, committing burglaries and dishing out hidings on a regular basis. This crime wave is probably fuelled by the fact that the town has more ice than a penguin's perineum. In fact, Moree's 'methidemic' is so bad that its garbage is routinely contaminated with thousands of used needles, leading local authorities to install special needle bins and run a publicity campaign called 'Be Sharp Safe' featuring a cartoon bee. Fortunately, Moree is home to artesian hot springs that locals claim have healing properties, which is particularly helpful for people trying to recover from knife wounds, track marks and other assorted injuries caused by living in Moree.

The 1965 Freedom Ride famously shone a light on the appalling state of Moree's race relations, including the segregation of the local swimming pool. Unfortunately, while the pool is now open to any local resident, it is still full of discarded syringes and the recipient of a code brown on an almost weekly basis. Moree is also known for its cotton-growing industry, which along with its rampant racism, meth addiction and incest makes it Australia's answer to Alabama.

ALSO KNOWN AS The Big M, Moron, Booree, More E.

Wat a crock of shit.. nearly every town I've been it's worser than Moree (Jiminy Sphincter, Moree)

Everyone has an opionion. A shame the authors is biasst (Gwen Clump, Moree)

Who ever wrote this is just looking for the attention Lol if ya from Moree ya knows True and What Isn't also they would have had to been from Moree lol porn just a really really dumb fuck wit. (Chrystal Meff, Moree)

i wonder what SHIT town the Author lives in—because he just about rights every town off. For your knowledge i live in Yamba voted BEST (Percy Grogan, Yamba)

Armidale voted the 21st most intelligent community in the world. So stick that up your arse after you pull your head out of it . (Bobert Nangs, Armidale)

Who ever wrote this woparse is af...ktard (Ricky Fapflaps, Armidale)

Kempsey

A rusting hulk of a town halfway between Brisbane and Sydney, Kempsey exists purely as a service centre for nearby places where people actually want to go. The town is so shit that it was not only bypassed by the rebuilt Pacific Highway but given a five-kilometre radius at a cost of millions of dollars to be on the safe side. The new bypass includes the longest bridge in Australia—the government broke a national record just to avoid the place.

Kempsey is renowned around the country for its two biggest exports: Slim Dusty and meth. The prolific Slim Dusty released over a hundred punishing albums of country songs, also known as 'bush ballads' or 'purdy music sounds'. An estimated tens of thousands of sheilas have been impregnated by their brothers to a Dusty ditty. Kempsey is also famous for recording the highest 'no' vote in the 1967 referendum to recognise the Indigenous as actual people, adding rampant racism to its redneck rap sheet.

Kempsey is also well known as a crime-ridden craphole where even second-floor windows are adorned with iron bars, or 'Kempsey curtains'. The town is crawling with gronks bricking each other, thugs mugging people on the railway pedestrian bridge and stray dogs picking through garbage. Activities for kids include asking strangers for ciggies, getting pregnant during P.E. class, and jumping off bridges into the turd-riddled river while trying not to land on the artificial reef made of dumped shopping trolleys and stolen dirt bikes. As if the crime wasn't enough, Kempsey is also built on a flood plain so often finds itself underwater, which is when local yokels usually have their annual bath.

ALSO KNOWN AS K-Town, Hempsey, Crapsey, Dumpsey, Crimesey, Cuntsey.
MOST FAMOUS PERSON Slim Dusty, who was sued multiple times for false advertising given that he was neither slim nor dusty. To be fair, 'Ruddy Paunch', while accurate, isn't a great cowboy name.

Taree

Taree is synonymous with oysters, arseholes and unemployment. The town's primary produce is commemorated by the Big Oyster, an attempted tourist attraction that was originally an unsuccessful restaurant and souvenir shop but has since converted to a car dealership because nobody visits Taree. With a mouthful of windows that look disturbingly like teeth, the yonic monument is reviled by residents and commonly referred to as the 'Big Mistake', a nickname that also works for Taree itself as well as each of its inhabitants.

Aside from being infested with disgusting slimy molluscs, Taree's Manning River hosts rowing and powerboat events in which rich people from other towns compete to slalom between semi-submerged syringes, turds and carcasses as quickly as possible. The town's other major event is the Taree Show, featuring such popular activities as cattle judging—the swimsuit section is a particular local favourite.

When they're not busy shucking shellfish or lusting over livestock, Taree's unemployed inhabitants enjoy bumming darts in supermarket car parks, chugging grog from paper bags in the park, or just staying home and honing their domestic violence skills. A popular local tradition is pelting passing buses with rocks and bottles, then doing the same to emergency services when they turn up. Tareeans also enjoy a spot of segregation, with the Indigenous community banished to one side of town and shunned when they enter pubs. When you arrive in Taree, remember to set your watch back 80 years.

ALSO KNOWN AS The Big Mistake, Blahree, Tareeks.
DID YOU KNOW? Taree is surrounded by satellite towns with stupid names like Cundletown, Cedar Party and Old Bar.

Forster-Tuncurry 

Despite sounding like an overweight detective on a mediocre British dramedy, Forster-Tuncurry is actually a dodgy little beach resort town on the Mid North Coast. A ratshit Gold Coast for yobs from Newcastle, Forster-Tuncurry resembles the Glitter Strip if you deleted all the nightlife, entertainment and anything remotely interesting. Rather than existing as a single shithole, Forster-Tuncurry is actually a pair of conjoined shitters linked by an eyesore of a concrete bridge across Wallis Lake, a double disappointment for anyone foolish enough to book a holiday.

Forster-Tuncurry is a major producer of oysters, which might explain the rampant horniness among the elderly population, who are just as aroused by

This is so dis hurting THAT YOU ALL CAN SAY NOT GOOD THINGS ABOUT KEMPSEY LOOK IN YOUR OWN BACKYARD BE FOR YOU SAYING AT ALL (Geraldine Jockstrap, Kempsey)

WTF is this billshit. This reeks of some mindless entitled milenial that stumbled on a cliche machine and knew how to hit the go button. Well done possum. Like most youngsters you're probably to fat and lazy to even make it up here for a swim. Blow it out your arse. (Julio Junta, Port Macquarie)

What a load of bullshit your not just implying cesnock your implying the the hole hunter valley go walk down the street with a sign on your head and see how the convicts ancestors and red necks will treat your shit (Gus Sluice, Cessnock)

NO DIFFERENT TO ANY TOWN IN THE WORLD ,,
LIVE HERE AND THEN TELL ME ITS SHIT ,,
AINT GUNNA HAPPEN ,,
I BIN EAR FA 33 YEARS AND AINT GOEN NOWHERE ,,
PS IM NOT TELLIN BUT ME CAP LOCK IS
STUCK ON ,, (Bevan Flange, Cessnock)

aphrodisiac shellfish as they are by negative gearing and the twin towns' abundance of saggy skin. Ironically, during the summer tourist season Forster-Tuncurry's population swells like a Viagra-induced hard-on and, much like an older gentleman with an artificially induced stiffy, the towns struggle to deal with the sudden rush of excitement. Popular tourist activities include catching herpes from a tradie from Cessnock, stealing an old fart's mobility scooter or getting in a fistfight with a pelican.

TOWN SLOGAN Forster Makes Me Moister than an Oyster!
ALSO KNOWN AS Forced a Tongue Curry.
DID YOU KNOW? Tuncurry was actually settled by immigrants from Calcutta and the name references the proliferation of Indian restaurants that line the main street. Unfortunately, despite the name, it's nearly impossible to get a decent tikka masala in town.

Summer Bay

Sitting somewhere on the New South Wales coast, Summer Bay is the quintessential Aussie seaside town, featuring stunning white sand beaches, a painfully Caucasian population and an average IQ in the double digits. It also features other shit town staples such as shirtless surfer morons with suspiciously crap tattoos, a depressed economy and an old loon who shouts unsolicited advice in impenetrable slang that nobody has used since Gallipoli.

Locals can often be found hanging around the only three places in town where anything actually happens: the surf club,

the cafe or the bait shop run by the aforementioned old loon. Residents of Summer Bay make up for this lack of local entertainment by rooting each other senseless. Luckily, Summer Bay features a suspiciously attractive population, something that is especially apparent when compared to the Morlocks and uggos that inhabit the likes of Yabbie Creek and Mangrove River. Consequently, many of Summer Bay's former residents often find themselves living in Hollywood or pesting around reality television shows in the hope that someone will subscribe to their OnlyFans page.

Despite its rather sunny appearance, Summer Bay has been the target of more catastrophes than an NRL team on a Mad Monday trip to Bali. Natural disasters include a flood, a mudslide, a caravan park explosion, a cyclone and even an earthquake. This doesn't count the sheer number of human disasters that seem to inhabit the town, including a raft of serial killers, sex pests and assorted drongos. Given the crime rate and the general level of calamity that befalls the average resident of Summer Bay, it's a small wonder that anyone would want to live there.

Summer Bay's reputation as a wedding destination has also taken a hit in recent years—most nuptials held there are seemingly overrun with deranged stalkers, irate exes and ghost dads. If you are considering getting hitched in Summer Bay, you are probably better off looking at Kabul if you want things to run smoothly.

TOWN SLOGAN Closer Each Day.
MOST FAMOUS PEOPLE Actors Isla Fisher, Melissa George, Chris Hemsworth, Heath Ledger, Dannii Minogue, Guy Pearce and Naomi Watts have all resided in this tiny town.

Maitland

Maitland spruiks itself as the 'first town of the Hunter Valley', a claim vigorously contested by Newcastle, which is a bit like two hobos fighting over a shit sandwich. The city was founded by notorious petty criminal and bigamist Molly Morgan, who was exiled to New South Wales before escaping and being sent back for another crime. While Newcastle was a favourite dumping ground for Britain's undesirables, Maitland was where Newcastle sent theirs, making it basically a convict colony convict colony. The

Maitland's trial of a Venetian-style canal system sadly proved unpopular with locals.

settlement was built on the banks of the massively flood-prone Hunter River and has sprawled over the top of old coalmines, so is an ideal place to live if you enjoy choking on coaldust, falling into abandoned mine shafts or drowning in your living room.

Maitland's premier event is the annual Hunter Valley Steamfest, which famously features a race between a steam train and a biplane. The biplane almost always wins, but only because the train is invariably relieved of its wheels by locals and left resting on cinder blocks before it can reach the finish line. The city's rugby league team is the Pickers, named for the local tradition of digging sooty boogers out of their snouts mid-match and smearing them on opponents' jerseys.

For sightseers, Maitland is home to an unparalleled array of shit monuments. The Black Boy is a fibreglass replica of an American 'lawn jockey', a racist relic proudly displayed on the main street. 'Fetch Boy' is a statue of a human-dog hybrid picking up its own turd having just taken a shit in public, a pointed critique of Maitlanders' hygiene habits. Appropriately, the bogan-infested city also hosts the Big Ugg Boots, a supersized shrine to Australia's favourite sheepskin skank shoes (most of which are actually made in Third World sweatshops from rat hides and recycled pubes).

Maitland: first in the Hunter Valley . . . for floods, subsidence and casual racism.

ALSO KNOWN AS Maito, Masturbaitland, No Matesland.

MOST FAMOUS PERSON Bare-knuckle boxer Les Darcy. To this day, Maitlanders honour

Darcy by bare-knuckle boxing strangers in the street.

Cessnock

Sat on the edge of the Hunter Valley (so named because locals hunt visitors), Cessnock is essentially Newcastle's Logan, or Maitland's Maitland. The city's name is an old Scottish word, 'cess' meaning 'toilet' and 'nock' meaning 'hole'. Its official slogan is 'Mines, Wines and People', which is a polite way of saying 'Air Pollution, Alcoholism and Dickheads'.

With coalmining in decline, Cessnock has been forced to turn to alternative industries such as fish and chips, supplying pingas to Newcastle Knights players, and wine—i.e. churning out goon for other bogan towns. The region's mine-adjacent vineyards are the perfect place to try some semillon

with an aroma of carbon and an aftertaste of cancer. Brimming with bored bogans, bursting with bewildered boomers and surrounded by soot-coated wineries, Cessnock is what would happen if you dumped Morwell in the middle of Tuscany.

Cessnock is also the proud home of a major prison, complete with the country's first purpose-built maximum-security

Who the fuck are you??? You wouldn't know your asshole from a hole in the ground. How can you judge a beautiful city like this as harshly as you have…& yet someone as qualified as Lonely Planet ranks Newcastle as one of...if not the best city in Australia!! FUCK OFF... in capital letters!!! (Sue Belcher, Newcastle)

Mate I no know we're you come from but please not come to newcaste if you do would be a real good fucking idea to shout that mouth of your and not post shit I grow up there a cunts like you should not talk about things u no fuck all about go back to prison (Graham Arsenic, Newcastle)

That's disgusting!!! My hubby my dog & I live in Woy Woy & we are lovely people who help others, go to Church, believe in God & help our friends plus people we don't know well & they help us too so shut the fuck up!!! ('Torchy' Wagstaff, Woy Woy)

What a sick piece of gardage (Pam Pillory, Woy Woy)

unit for sex pests. Consequently, Necknock is populated by numerous nonces prowling around the Turner Park toilets, as well as a stellar line-up of crackhead car thieves, drunk deadbeat dads with domestic violence convictions, and inbred rednecks wielding homemade weapons. In 1820, approximately 50 per cent of Cessnock's population were convicts. Two hundred years later, the ratio is about the same.

TOWN SLOGAN Mines, Wines and Crime.
ALSO KNOWN AS Cesspool, Cesspit, Necknock, Headknock, Thethnock, Methnock, Cessrock, Pestnock, Incestnock.
MOST FAMOUS PERSON Andrew Johns, eighth rugby league immortal and notorious pinga rat.

Woy Woy ☮

The witticisms 'God's waiting room' and 'the world's only above-ground cemetery' have been co-opted to describe numerous retirement towns but were originally coined by comedian Spike Milligan for the Central Coast geriatric camp of Woy Woy.

Despite his insults, the Indian-born Anglo-Irishman is celebrated as a deity in Woy Woy as the only person of note ever to pay any attention to the town. In a sort of mass-scale Stockholm syndrome, Woy Woy honours its tormentor with a permanent exhibition at the local library and, formerly, an annual festival. Milligan also has a bridge named after him in the town, after Woy Woy took literally his suggestion that they 'build a bridge and get over it'. Fittingly,

Woy Woy's only celebrity was not even a resident but was a frequent visitor, as the illiterate cultural wasteland was the ideal place for a writer trying to escape attention. At the time, not only did Woy Woyans have no idea who Spike Milligan was, they didn't even know what a book was—half of which remains the case.

Sadly, the comatose coffin-dodger paradise that Milligan knew is fast disappearing as property developers and hipsters alike invade at a great rate, replacing all of the derelict weatherboard and fibro shacks with apartment blocks, multistorey mansions, New Age shops peddling bullshit for post-menopausal hippies, and pretentious cafes that serve soup in teapots. Even the prince of put-downs himself would be hard-pressed to sum up the bona fide bastion of wank that Woy Woy has become. The town is still part of the Centrelink Coast, however, so there's a decent chance of getting beaten up at a train station, shopping centre or yoga class. Get bashed while you still can!

ALSO KNOWN AS WW, Dub Dub, The Peninsula, Woy & Woy, 2woy, Double Woy, Dos Woy, the Woys, Woy Fucking Woy, Why Why, Mount Druitt's Retirement Home.

DID YOU KNOW? A popular Central Coast saying is 'Get along to Ettalong'. Lesser-known variations include 'Puff a joint at Buff Point', 'Get your bong ready for Long Jetty', 'Try chroming at Wyoming', 'Stroke your banana at Copacabana', 'Get put in a coma in Tacoma', and 'Get stabbed 57 times in the face in Wyong'.

only some pollution riden city clicker would right that (Corey Chutney, Lithgow)

To all knockers of my penrith city thanks all of you must have no life if taking time to discuss this shit city according to all of you i don't have the time to discus the great areas were all you are came on have the balls to tell us we're you leave north south east for sure no west people like all of you are not allowed in a family honest humble city as penrith I wish all of you knocker a fuckin shit day (Lawrence Hills-Hoist, Penrith)

Katoomba

Katoomba is the name of a crater on Mars. It's also the name of a crater in the Blue Mountains that masquerades as a town. Renowned for its miserable grey skies and bracing chill, the frigid shithole is cold enough to freeze the balls off a brass junkie.

If you've ever been to Lithgow, picture Lithgow. That's Katoomba. The only real difference is the people: instead of hillbilly shard monkeys, Katoomba is infested by wannabe poets, artists, musicians, environmentalists, retirees and other assorted dole bludgers—as well as hillbilly shard monkeys. Increasingly, Katoomba is also being invaded by cashed-up Sydneysiders and pseudo-celebrities, as well as pretentious hipsters opening the type of cafes where you can get a gluten-free panini served on an old hubcap with a side of COVID-denying conspiracy theories.

As the closest thing in the Blue Mountains to civilisation, Katoomba is inundated with tourists on any given day—mostly white-haired walking-stick-wielders shuffling about aimlessly in gigantic groups. One of the most popular sights is the Three Sisters, a trio of sandstone shafts and also something you can enjoy at the local brothel.

Katoomba's primary event is the Winter Magic Festival, an excuse for ageing hippies to slap on a masquerade mask, smoke a blunt and bang a belly dancer. The confused Katoombans also hold a Christmas festival called Yulefest in the middle of the year, a recurring mistake caused by the region's permanent winter. Outside of event season, there is so little to do that residents are forced to resort to drastic measures like commuting to Penrith.

Blacktown

Sporting a racist name, an abundance of empty schools and hordes of housos, the City of Blacktown is a veritable smorgasbord of shit. The Western Sydney LGA is crammed with crap suburbs including Mount Druitt (commonly called Mount Druggitt), Shalvey (Shankvey), Doonside (Goonside) and Rooty Hill (Shagger's Ridge, Humpy Hump or Fucky Mound). Thanks to its rougher bits—locally referred to in hushed tones as 'the areas'—Blacktown is Australia's murder, gun crime and 'fleeing the cops on a stolen unregistered dirt bike' capital. Blacktown's rugby league team is called the Workers, which is ironic because no one there has a job. Aside from unemployment, the most popular occupations in Slacktown are trying to crack the NRL (even though you are 32), working on your mixtape and stealing each other's stuff. On the plus side, housing in Blacktown is cheap by Sydney standards because no one wants to live there.

Of all the lumps that make up the Blacktown turd, the worst is objectively Mount Druitt. Despite its name, Mount Druitt is not a mountain, adding false advertising to its long list of common local crimes that also includes urban warfare, wanton vandalism and having a rat's tail. Mount Druitt is actually a hole, which is the opposite of a mountain.

Mounty County is also the proud hometown of OneFour, a try-hard gangsta rap group so shit they were banned from touring in Australia. OneFour are popular with people who consider hoodies formal attire, punching strangers a fun activity and a twelve-pack of Woodstock breakfast. The only positive of Mount Druitt's youth is that unlike the population of Melbourne during a pandemic, they have no problem with wearing face masks in public.

There have been several attempts to rename Blacktown something less overtly racist, but despite the suggestion of several fitting alternatives—Cracktown, Gronkville, Sydney's Anus—the efforts failed as the majority of residents are illiterate and couldn't spell any of the proposed names.

TOWN SLOGAN Get a Smackdown in Blacktown!
ALSO KNOWN AS Stabtown, Cracktown, Smacktown, Slacktown.
DID YOU KNOW? Mount Druitt was famously shamed in the SBS documentary *Struggle Street*, which a furious Blacktown mayor labelled 'poverty porn'. One participant was aggrieved that the show included footage of her husband farting. The show's critics were apparently unaware that *Struggle Street* was a promotional piece produced by the Mount Druitt Tourism Board, and that several drug deals and at least three murders were carefully edited out of the final cut.

Parramatta

The bit of Sydney that the rest of Sydney prefers to pretend doesn't exist, Parramatta is a sprawling suburban shitscape dotted with RSLs, shopping centres and copy-pasted townhouses. The city is regarded as the CBD of Greater Western Sydney, or in other words, the capital of Shitsville. It is Australia's oldest inland European settlement, having been settled before explorers discovered the vast myriad of better places to live. In its early days, Parramatta gained the nickname of 'Australia's cradle city' due to all the teen pregnancies. It is now home to the New South Wales Police Force, who go where they're needed most.

Parramatta likes to boast about its 'vibrant culture', which is true if 'vibrant culture' means casual stabbings, flagrant drug

use and a CBD full of bands of roving junkies. Plans by the state government to relocate the Powerhouse Museum to Western Sydney have been mired in controversy, with many detractors suggesting that Parramatta will reject any attempt to instil culture there in much the same way that an organ donor's body rejects a pig heart as something that doesn't belong. In the meantime, Parramatta will have to make do with what has always passed for 'culture': a meat raffle at the RSL.

'Parramatta' translates to 'the place where the eels lie down', a reference to its awful NRL team. It's not surprising that the city identifies with a spineless bottom feeder most at home in stagnant water and sewers. The Eels have done Parramatta proud with a long history of mediocrity coupled with some truly memorable off-field incidents, including drug possession, road rage and consorting with bikies.

ALSO KNOWN AS Parra, Cradle City, Parismatta, Parra-doesn't-matter.

Northern Beaches ☮ 🥸 ʃ

Extending from Port Jackson to Broken Bay and taking in some of Sydney's most expensive shit suburbs such as Manly, Dee Why and Palm Beach, the Northern Beaches is a bastion of self-important snobbery with a side of paranoia.

The region is the natural habitat of some of the worst types of Sydneysiders: CEOs in board shorts, upper-class hipsters, Insta-sluts, trophy wives,

yoga-obsessed anti-vaxxers, baby boomer slumlords and Tony Abbott. It's also full of drongo surfer stereotypes who refuse to cross the bridge under any circumstances but will happily stab you for the perfect wave. Fortunately for the residents of the rest of Sydney, those who live on the 'Insular Peninsula' rarely travel south, acting like they are surrounded by an impenetrable moat rather than at the other end of the A8.

Despite its nauseatingly posh veneer, the Northern Beaches is actually a festering hotbed of crime, with offences ranging from rampant tax evasion to buying Paleo Pete books to the filming of *Home and Away*. It is also guilty of the heinous crime of almost touching the Central Coast—indeed, large chunks of the Northern Beaches are basically Gosford with more disposable income and less hepatitis.

ALSO KNOWN AS NB, the Insular Peninsula, Northern Bitches.

Inner West

Infested by well-heeled hipsters inexplicably fixated on drinking trendy coffee outside scummy cafes with crumbling cladding, gorging on expensive brunch at graffiti-coated eateries and buying daggy clothes from mouldy vintage stores, Sydney's Inner West is a loathsome region where carefully curated Third-World squalor masquerades as culture. The Inner West could equally be described as a shit version of London's East End or a war-torn ISIS enclave if terrorists had fedoras and flesh tunnels.

Less Chardonnay socialists and more craft beer Bolsheviks, the residents of the Inner West are obsessed with the obscure—obscure cuisine, obscure facial hair and obscure sexual manoeuvres that they learned from their last Pornhub binge. If you wake up next to a young lady sporting a handlebar moustache chafed red raw from performing a 'Reverse Tasmanian Devil', then chances are you're in Newtown.

The standard-issue uniform

of an Inner Westie includes some purely cosmetic eyewear, an ironic tattoo of a childhood cartoon character and a dodgy mo that looks like it belongs on a rock spider rather than a barista. Popular activities include complaining about white privilege while letting your parents pay your rent, claiming to be a 'male feminist' while maxing out your credit card on OnlyFans subscriptions, and foisting petitions to ban microagressions against little people on unsuspecting middle-class types.

Inevitably, the hipsters of Marrickville and Newtown will continue living lives of bourgeois excess until they settle down, move to a suburb full of people who do actual jobs, and have kids with old-fashioned names that sound like people who died while exploring the Congo.

Eastern Suburbs

Sydney's Eastern Suburbs is home to some of the world's most iconic beaches—unfortunately, it is also home to some of the world's biggest dickheads. Populated largely by the feckless offspring of investment bankers and property developers, the most popular activities in the Eastern Suburbs include taking Instagram photos of your acai bowl, working for your dad and claiming to be an 'entrepreneur' on dating apps. The average Eastern Suburbanite is easily identifiable by their gym-sculpted rig, a wardrobe slathered in Ralph Lauren Polo logos and a timepiece more expensive than a Campbelltown fibro.

The Eastern Suburbs' premier attraction is the world-famous Bondi Beach, a flog-frequented patch of sand usually covered with pasty British backpackers sunbaking themselves to the colour of burnt bacon and hoping to leave the Lucky Country with that most Australian of souvenirs, melanoma. The popular Bondi to Coogee coastal walk is great if you're keen to case some flash houses or fall off a cliff. While in town, watch the Sydney Roosters, who take advantage of their fans' natural proclivity towards financial fraud to be perennial contenders in the NRL (National Rort-the-salary-cap League).

Recently the locals have launched a campaign to ban trains and buses from the Eastern Suburbs in order to cut down on the number of peasants who can freely roam their well-appointed

Recreational sunburning on Bondi Beach.

streets. Who needs public transport when you have a Tesla powered solely by the owner's smug sense of self-satisfaction?

Sutherland Shire

Commonly called 'The Shire' like something out of a shit children's book, Sutherland Shire is home to sun-cooked surfies, image-obsessed idiots, Hillsong hillbillies and other types of the worst white people. A backwards country town stuck in a big city, it's like someone dropped Dubbo at the arse end of Botany Bay and told them to make the best of it. The only thing smaller than the mind of the average Shire resident is their steroid-atrophied gonads—considering the shrivelled raisins the average Cronullagator is working with, it's surprising that any of them are able to sire broods of illegitimate sprogs. Sutherland Shire is also home to the Sharks, a gang of bogans so feral that even the rest of the NRL thinks they are a bit much.

The area was immortalised in the terrible television series *The Shire*, a pseudo-reality show about a bunch of vapid nitwits with names like Rif-Raf, Michelka and Beckaa. Shire residents were outraged that Shire residents were portrayed accurately in the show and the mayor threatened to ban the production.

The jewel in The Shire's crown is Cronulla, a suburb most famous for its 2005 race riots in which throngs of flag-wearing rednecks took to the streets and beaches to bash brown people. Classy Cronullafornia is also home to a giant mural of Shannon Noll getting his nip out. Nearby Engadine is enshrined in folklore as the site of an alleged

fast-food faecal fiasco by a future prime minister. Arguably as significant as ScoMo's chocolate McFlurry was James Cook's first landing in Australia at Kurnell in 1770, which began the long tradition of immigrants arriving in The Shire only to be told to fuck off back to where they came from.

TOWN SLOGAN Far Kurnell!

ALSO KNOWN AS The Shire, The Shite, God's Country, Sufferland.

DID YOU KNOW? Sutherland Shire is home to Australia's only nuclear facility, which might explain all the fucking mutants who live there.

Campbelltown

Campbelltown is fully sick. Fully sick in that everyone there has type 2 diabetes, gout or hepatitis C. Campbelltonians have their residency revoked if they fail to register at least three positives in an STI test.

A Sydney satellite that wasn't flung far enough, the City of Campbelltown exists mainly as a place for Greater Sydney to store its most embarrassing residents out of sight of polite company. Common hobbies of Campbelltonians include hanging ciggies out of the gap where their front teeth used to be, begging for change at the station for a train they have no intention of catching, and slipping their electronic ankle bracelets to go and burn down a pub.

Among Campbelltown's worst suburbs is Airds, which has a primary school and a high school conveniently located next to a juvenile detention centre, allowing for a seamless

transition. The high school is Australia's only one with its own birthing unit, methadone clinic and parole office. Airds was named after Governor Lachlan Macquarie's wife, Elizabeth, who had AIDS.

The biggest event on the Campbelltown calendar is the Festival of Fisher's Ghost, when the hometown of serial killers Ivan Milat and Paula Denyer celebrates the murder of a local farmer by sacrificing a virgin to Satan. The arduous task of actually finding a virgin in Campbelltown begins the day after the festival and usually takes the entire year.

ALSO KNOWN AS C-Town, Crumbletown, Shambletown, Scandaltown, Criminaltown.
MOST FAMOUS PERSON Ivan Milat, Australia's lowest-rated tourist transport provider.

EVENT
BATHURST 1000

Held at the Mount Panorama Circuit in the eponymous shit town, the Bathurst 1000 is an annual orgy of car carnage that sees vast hordes of mechanophiles drink-drive from as far afield as Logan, Geelong and Penrith for a long weekend of cheering on their favourite international automobile manufacturing conglomerate. The options are Holden or Ford, and you must choose one. You don't need to know why—you just need to buy a decal of Calvin pissing on whichever one you didn't pick.

In an effort to reduce the booze-fuelled anarchy, authorities have imposed a limit of one box of grog per drongo per day, barely enough to keep the average Australian male awake. Enterprising yobbos have

taken to burying crates of VB months prior to the Great Race and digging them up on the big day in the most bogan treasure hunt possible. Popular side events include blowing up toilet blocks, firebombing ice-cream trucks, and beating up people who like the wrong type of car.

Traditionally dominated by the intense rivalry between Ford and Holden, Bathurst has recently plummeted in cultural significance due to the latter's demise. Holden was replaced for the 2021 edition by Chevrolet, a brand with about as much relevance to Australians as the concept of shame or the phrase 'drinking in moderation'. It remains to be seen if the event's celebrated '*Hunger Games* for hillbillies' vibe will survive the setback.

Goulburnites prefer their sheep like their sexual partners: girthy, unshaven and possibly diseased.

MILAT MILE

SYDNEY TO MELBOURNE

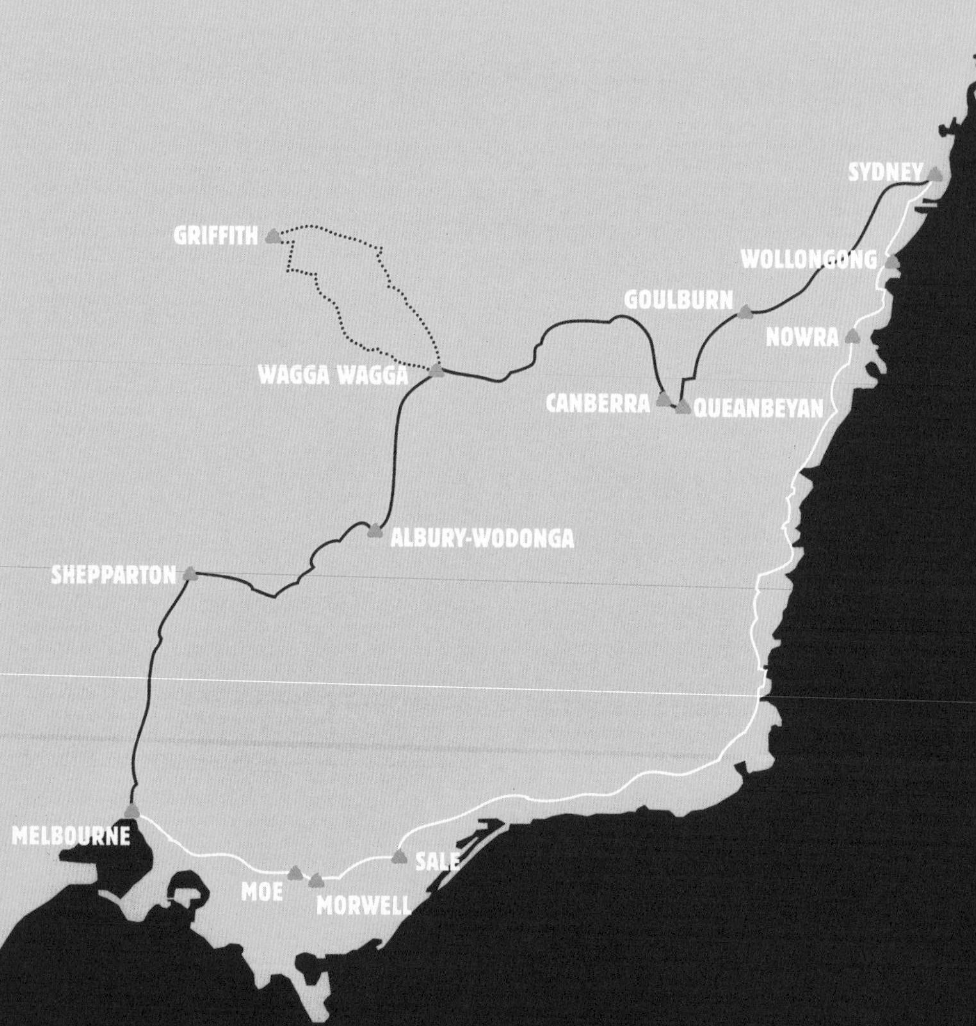
SYDNEY
GRIFFITH
WOLLONGONG
GOULBURN
NOWRA
WAGGA WAGGA
CANBERRA
QUEANBEYAN
ALBURY-WODONGA
SHEPPARTON
MELBOURNE
SALE
MOE
MORWELL

ROUTE NOTES

COASTAL ROUTE

WOLLONGONG* Newcastle for people who have given up (see Dapto, page 88).

NOWRA* An acronym for 'Number Of Welfare Recipients Astronomical'.

SALE (page 95)

MORWELL (page 97)

MOE (page 100)

MELBOURNE* Home to horrible people like hipsters, craft beer wankers, militant vegans and AFL fans (pages 102–110).

INLAND ROUTE

GOULBURN (page 89)

QUEANBEYAN (page 92)

CANBERRA* Pyongyang in the bush.

WAGGA WAGGA* So much ice they named it twice.

OPTIONAL DETOUR: GRIFFITH (page 94)

ALBURY-WODONGA* Twin turds in a shit sandwich.

SHEPPARTON* A portmanteau of 'sheep' and 'methamphetamine'.

* Reviewed in *Sh*t Towns of Australia*

Dapto

Dapto is shit. Wollongong is shit. As the worst part of Wollongong, Dapto is a shit within a shit—a *Shitception*, if you will. If someone ate a shit and then shat it out again, Dapto would be that second shit. In mathematical terms, shit times shit equals Dapto. It's the shit in a shit pie if the pastry was also shit.

One of the shittest things about Dapto is the people. Dapto's dubious denizens include deadshits, deros, drongos, dipshits, drug dealers and dropkicks. The derelict dump competes with Albion Park Rail for the title of Greater Wollongong's bogan capital, with flannos, trackies and bikie beards adorning every resident (both genders). Dapto is surrounded by suburbs with names like Kanahooker and Whoresley, in reference to the local women. It also features a number of streets that hint at its unsavoury reputation, including Bong Bong Road, Compton Street and Coward Punch Terrace.

Dapto's premier tourist attractions are the Dapto Dogs, Dapto Traino and Dapto Leagues Club. The greyhound club's dogs are honed for racing by being released on Bong Bong Road, where they are forced to survive by chasing down and eating pedestrians. The train station was famously the inspiration for animated YouTube duo *Damo and Darren*, the answer to the question 'What would happen if Beavis and Butthead were Australian and addicted to crack?' Another local attraction is Mullet Creek (named after Dapto's prevalent hairstyle), a popular spot for kids to jump off a bridge and break their legs on a dead cow.

ALSO KNOWN AS Crapto, Dumpto.

Goulburn

A reluctant piss stop for travellers on the Hume Highway, Goulburn was proclaimed Australia's first inland city in 1863—although it was quickly stripped of this title due to being less of a city and more of a shithole. It was once again proclaimed a city in 1885, making it the only place in Australia to have been declared a city twice. Although it has not been declared a city since, it continues to be declared a shithole at every opportunity.

Goulburn's best claim to fame

is the world's largest concrete sheep (see page 84 and above), an achievement approximately on par with doing the biggest poo in your pants. Covered from head to hoof in flabby folds, the Big Merino looks more like a malignant tumour than a farm animal. Unbelievably, the monstrous monument was modelled on a real ram, proving that the livestock in Goulburn are just as inbred as the locals. Fun fact: the Big Merino is believed to be the only building in Australia with visible gonads.

Goulburn's next major tourist attraction is the Goulburn Correctional Centre, the highest-security prison in Australia. This makes Goulburn the home of some of the country's most reprehensible individuals including terrorists, mass murderers and NRL players. It's also home to the New South Wales Police Academy, located a short distance from the prison, which is convenient given that half of its graduates eventually end up there.

With mass amounts of fuck-all to do in Goulburn, local losers are forced to resort to such tedious tasks as playing twelve-fingered banjo ballads, doing endless laps of Auburn Street or trying to get into the Dirty Bird (a.k.a. Flamingos nightclub) in their pyjamas. The city is also known as Gouldilocks because it's always either too hot or too cold. Other problems include constant droughts, relentless wind, a pervasive stench of horse shit, and being close to Canberra.

TOWN SLOGAN Goulburn it Down!

ALSO KNOWN AS G-Town, the Burn, Gouldilocks, Goblin, Holeburn, Gaolburn, Doleburn, Gronkburn.

MOST FAMOUS PERSON Todd Carney, a one-man gronknado whose CV includes being sacked by three NRL clubs, several drink-driving charges, being banned from his hometown for a year after jumping on a car and smashing a shop door, and being photographed appearing to piss into his own mouth. The latter incident didn't shake Goulburn's love of Toddy—most residents were just impressed that someone could have the hand–eye coordination to be able to pull it off.

Queanbeyan

Situated just outside of the Australian Capital Territory by careful design, Queanbeyan is the bit of Canberra that the ACT didn't want. When the ACT was established in 1911, the border was carefully drawn around the pre-existing village of Queanbeyan so as not to sully the new territory with a shit town.

Queanbeyan has since been subsumed by Canberra's urban sprawl but the ACT's borders have not moved to accommodate it, as experts fear moving such a shithole inside the territory's limits could plunge the capital, and by extension the country, into a deep depression—both the economic type and the other kind. Indeed, the only winner in such a scenario would be New South Wales.

If you thought Canberra was dull, Queanbeyan is a masterclass in mediocrity. Commonly called Queanbangers or Quang Dang by locals but known in Canberra as 'the Hole', Queanbeyan is basically Canberra's foreskin, and most Canberrans would love nothing more than to whip out the scalpel and ring the rabbi. The Choirboys song 'Struggle Town', in which the vocalist declares he's getting out and never going back, was famously written about Queanbeyan.

Composed of boarded-up buildings, coated in dead grass and cloaked in the smell of burning petrol, Queanbeyan would be considered uninhab-itable by normal people. The only lifeforms willing to live in such a squalid shit-sty are the region's biggest bogans, the kind of Culture Kings–kitted fuck-knuckles

Don't disrespect The Gong ya fuckin dog. I bet you're too pissweak to even meet me at puckeys reserve later and have a fisty all night. (Dennis Durry, Wollongong)

Whoever wrote this is obviously gone blind from wanking himself. (Simon Smegma, Nowra)

Well woopedo all go piss off at your own shit hole and f CK just because there is no jobs don't mean there are no good people there you pricks that don't support little towns wonder why tar and cement soul less pricks (Chuck Colostomy, Goulburn)

goulburn is not a shit town ,it has a great dignity add pride and so do our people how dare all you dispicable negative humans get a hold of you hate emotions and go and educatebto the area stop bei a whinging bullshit dribbling and go and piss somewhere else you bunch of sproggs (Barry Budgie-Smuggler, Goulburn) so aggravated by the tedium of living in Queanboring that they embark on a weekly pilgrimage to Canberra's city centre to grope uni students and coward-punch bureaucrats. Clearly, the Choirboys were bang on.

ALSO KNOWN AS QB, Qbyn, Queanbo, Queen Bee, Queen Bean, The Bean, Q-Town, Quimbeyan, Queanbangers, Quangers, Quang Dang, Screambeyan, Queefbeyan, Queanboring, Queanbehole, The Hole, Struggle Town, Canberra East.

MOST FAMOUS PERSON Former F1 driver Mark Webber, who learned how to race cars so he could drive away from Queanbeyan as quickly as possible.

Griffith

The regional shithole of Griffith was populated by Italian immigrants from its earliest days. Consequently, Gritaly is now infested with more Italian stereotypes than a pizza shop mascot convention: pasta chefs, Catholics, soccer hooligans, fascists, people walking around shouting 'mamma mia!' all the time, and—like Italian icons Mario and Luigi—tradies on shrooms. Naturally, Griffith is also synonymous with the Italian mafia, organised crime and mysterious disappearances. In fact, the nearby Necricon Swamp is so named because of all the bodies that keep being fished out of it. As well as Italians, Griffith features a growing population of Indian-Australians, affectionately known by locals as 'fully Sikh cunts'.

Griffith sits on the Kidman Way, a famous rural route (not to be confused with Nicole Kidman, a famous Urban root). The city is a service centre for the irrigation industry, which basically involves slurping up water from the country's dying rivers and selling it back to the government to put back in the rivers. Irrigation is also used for the area's vast vineyards (grape plantations) and 'vineyards' (cannabis plantations).

The profusion and proximity of wineries and pot farms is highly convenient for tourists, as the only possible way to enjoy Griffith is by being both drunk and high for the entire duration of their visit.

Griffith's attractions include irrigation channels brimming with broken bottles, syringes and the odd mobster who should have kept his mouth shut; a plethora of pokies; and a lake filled with toxic algae, which has been touted as a cause of the city's ridiculously high rate of motor neurone disease (seven times the national average). In 2010, Griffith got its first traffic lights. Next on the Grillbillies' wishlist are flush toilets, the internet and literacy.

ALSO KNOWN AS Griff, Griffo, G-Town, G-Hole, Graples, Griffilth, Gritaly.
DID YOU KNOW? The highlight of Griffith's calendar is an Italian sausage festival, which celebrates both the city's ethnic heritage and its chronic gender imbalance.

Sale

Sale was originally named 'Flooding Creek' after some dimwit decided to knock up a town in the middle of a swamp at the confluence of several major

waterways, then was surprised when the place duly flooded. The town was later renamed Sale in honour of locals' habit of selling anything not nailed down to pay for their next piss-up, a tradition that continues to this day.

Sale's most notable landmark is the La Trobe Swing Bridge, Australia's largest outdoor venue for wife-swapping gatherings. Along with the town's carp-infested canal, the crusty old contraption was constructed in the 1880s after the local brains trust tried to turn the town into a trading port. The plan was unsuccessful on account of Sale being shit, not to mention 30 kilometres inland.

Popular activities in Sale include walking at a brisk pace, hiffing shopping trolleys into the canal, and lapsing into a coma due to stultifying boredom. Sale is so notoriously boring that it has recently become Victoria's ice capital, as developing a crippling drug addiction is about the only thing that can make the Gippsland shitter tolerable.

Not content with frequent floods and rampant drug addiction, Sale also celebrates vaunted local founding father and piece of shit Angus McMillan with a sculpture commemorating his vital contributions to the Gippsland massacres. The appropriately hideous lump of rocks and concrete was apparently inspired by McMillan's treasured hessian sack of human skulls that he kept as a charming keepsake of his killings. Locals have resisted calls to tear down the loathsome monument, supporting the theory that the further east you go in Gippsland, the redder the neck.

ALSO KNOWN AS Stale.

DID YOU KNOW? English novelist Anthony Trollope visited Sale in 1872 and commented on the town's 'innumerable hotels', which was presumably meant as a compliment given his surname.

Morwell

Strategically hidden in the impenetrable smog of the Latrobe Valley, Morwell is a dull and depressing dump of a town that apparently exists purely to poison its residents. The town is surrounded by coal-fired power plants and mines that pollute the air and destroy the planet so Melburnians can enjoy uninterrupted access to Pornhub. The Hazelwood open-cut mine fire of 2014 blanketed Morwell in a thick layer of smoke, choking the local population—but improving

the scenery dramatically. Morwell is also handy to Australia's largest paper mill, which regularly makes the entire Latrine Valley smell like someone just sharted (which, given Morwellians' hygiene habits, they probably did). In most shit towns, sucking on bumpers made from scavenged ciggie butts is the preferred method of contracting herpes and lung cancer at the same time—in Morwell, locals need only walk outside and inhale. This makes Morwell's name rather ironic, as people who live there are actually substantially *less* well.

Unsurprisingly, the only people willing to live in such a soul-crushing suck shack are the sort of human detritus who have been jettisoned from respectable

Who ever wrote this article is a complete waste of sperm and probably a fucking keyboard warrior who probably still gets breast feed none of they have said is true (Greta Goon, Queanbeyan)

Profound ridden arse rapping nutter.
(Doug Dero, Wagga Wagga)

Whoever has written this nasty piece may u rot in the nericon river.
Do not come here
U r not welcome
U have brought nothing to this town
Hope u get corona virus
U narrowminded prick
We brought this town to fruitation
Do not let me c u drink our wine and enjoy our food
May u choke on it if u do (Chum Flanno, Griffith)

society. The Bairnsdale train line cuts between the town centre and Centrelink, creating an unusual scenario in which both sides of the tracks are the wrong side. Dumped mattresses, piles of used nappies and discarded sharps line the streets, and there are more couches in front yards than in houses. The comatose CBD consists of welfare services, two-dollar shops and abandoned buildings, the only activity being criminals visiting the justice precinct for processing and the odd ice zombie staggering across an empty road. The town is so dire that even its deadshit kids quickly tire of chucking mainies and instead head off to try to sneak into a bar in nearby Traralgon. Any place that drives someone to visit Traralgon is truly hell on earth.

ALSO KNOWN AS Poorwell, Morhell, Morhole, Morsmell, Morbowel, Mordor.

MOST FAMOUS PEOPLE Peter Siddle, famous vegan cricketer notorious for his consumption of up to twenty bananas a day, proving that Morwellians really struggle to say 'when' regardless of whether it's a toot on the see-through didgeridoo or Donkey Kong's favourite snack.

Moe

If Australia were a Monopoly board, the Latrobe Valley would definitely be the brown squares. Among the Smelly Valley's chief latrines is Moe, a shit town extraordinaire that ticks every box on the shit list: from drug and crime problems, massive unemployment, constant rain and air pollution to a sex pest–heavy

population that sifts about town in the traditional local attire of pyjamas and puffer vests.

Pronounced 'Mowee', 'Moe' is an old Indigenous word meaning 'shithole'. Appropriately, it shares its name with the most depressed character on *The Simpsons*, as well as a Japanese term for an unhealthy sexual attraction to underage cartoon characters. 'Moe' is also a well-known acronym for 'Moccasins On Everyone', though an equally accurate version would be 'Meth Overdoses Everyday'. In 2007 it was proposed that the town change its name from Moe to Moet to mooch off the reputation of the famous champagne brand, the sort of bogan logic that leads people to name their unplanned newborns Chardonnay or Schapelle and expect them not to become strippers or drug mules. Unfortunately, the plan was shot down by a section of angry locals who felt that aligning with a classy product like champagne would give visitors the wrong impression of Moe. It was then proposed renaming the town to something more fitting, like Monster Energy Mango Loco, but Monster declined to be involved because being associated with Moe would be bad for their image.

Moe was founded as a swampy gold diggers' piss stop, a suitably miserable origin for a seriously miserable town. This history is immortalised at Old Gippstown, a historical park that tries to make locals feel better by pretending that living in squalor is novel and fun. Visitors to Old Gippstown can see a goldminer's meth lab, Australia's first Centrelink and the first place someone successfully made love to an ugg boot. Today, the town has barely changed—it can be hard to tell where the primitive shacks of Old Gippstown end and the primitive shacks of 'modern' Moe begin.

M.O.E.—Move Over Ethiopia!

ALSO KNOWN AS Motown, Moccasin City.

Frankston

Situated in Melbourne's sphincter, Frankston is known as 'the gateway to the Mornington Peninsula' by people who don't realise that any trip down the M11 is almost certain not to involve an offramp in Frankghanistan. Given the habits of Frankstoners, a more accurate slogan would be 'the gateway to the morning-after pill'. Indeed, the suburb's nickname

Franga—also slang for condom—is extremely ironic as people who live there think using protection involves carrying knuckledusters and 'contraception' is the name of a Leonardo DiCaprio movie. On the other hand, Franga is an appropriate name because Frankston is also used to gather up all the gross shit you don't want making another human being.

Frankston North (a.k.a. 'The Pines') is the proverbial pube in the poo stew, the part of Frankston that even Frankstoners make Frankston jokes about. The Pines boasts a bounty of rub-and-tug joints, endless traffic chicanes and roundabouts to entertain street racers, and ample outdoor spaces for students of rival high schools to engage in fights. Not far away are the nightlife hotspots of the train station (with a free hep-C screening clinic usefully located across the road) and the hospital emergency department. Amid all of the effluent is the affluent enclave of Olivers Hill, where Frankston keeps its minority population of rich bastards conveniently grouped for burglary purposes.

Despite the flesh-eating bacteria in the water, Frankston Beach is a popular social spot for shitfaced sex pests and other miscellaneous maniacs. For eleven years Frankston residents showcased their expertise at manipulating powdery substances with Australia's biggest sandcastle competition, where locals created massive sand sculptures depicting their favourite things, such as giant dongs, crack pipes and Centrelink application forms. The event was moved to a new location in 2018 after a judge was pricked by a used needle embedded in a mermaid.

ALSO KNOWN AS Franga, Frangers, Frangtown, Funkytown, Franky, Frankhole, Frankstoned, Gangston, Wankston, Skankston, Shankston, Stabston, Gronkston, Frankenstein, Frankghanistan, Dandenong With a Beach, Moe By the Bay, Centrelink by the Sea.

DID YOU KNOW? As well as a wide variety of deros and dropkicks, Frankston is also famous for its wide variety of serial killers. Frankston has even had a transgender serial killer, like something out of a J.K. Rowling novel. In fact, Frankston is named after Frank 'the Al Fresco Murderer' Butler, Australia's first serial killer.

Dandenong

Dandenong is known for its 'culture', which is a quaint euphemism for violent crime, drugs, drunks, gangs, hoons and housos. The suburb is also famous for its diversity: in the same street you could eat Afghani, Indian, Albanian, Chinese or African food; buy some counterfeit clothing, a rug or a *Wiggles*-branded knuckleduster; or get stabbed with a knife, screwdriver or a crudely fashioned shank. The variety is endless! In fact, Dandenong is so ethnically diverse that One Nation voters and Queenslanders have been known to spontaneously combust upon setting foot there.

Widely considered to be the worst bit of Melbourne (a bold claim for a city that also contains Frankston and Cranbourne), Dandenong is somehow worse than its awful reputation. Popular pastimes include ram-raiding pharmacies, assaulting the

WTFIs wrong with some people ,If you don't like Not well or the Latrobe valley Just stay the Fuck away We don't need you here and you won't be missed , . (Dazza Gunt, Morwell)

some people omg not as bad as this is making it out to be sirusly Tafe Gippsland in morwell Anglicare and Barry street quotom lots more Bev's World of Dolls the plaza church's shit load hairs dresses lots shops shit load not just one lol workshops opshops list gose on planty to do if ya not looking for the worst and look at the positive stuff (Basil Moist, Morwell) elderly and a spot of recreational arson. If that's all a bit hectic for you then you could always wind down by visiting a makeshift brothel in a tent in a park.

Loitering menacingly on the outskirts of Melbourne, Dandenong is in many ways a forgotten suburb, cut off from the city by shit public transport connections. Despite this, most Melburnians would argue that it's still too close and would be quite happy for all roads leading in and out of the Nong to be ripped up and replaced with some sort of wall or moat. If you must visit, we suggest you pass through like a dodgy vindaloo.

ALSO KNOWN AS The Nong, Dandebong, Dandenang, Dandewrong, Dandruff.

Toorak

A bastion of entitled snobs since the 1880s, Toorak is synonymous with black Range Rovers, vaginal rejuvenation and old-money toffs. Comprised of tree-lined streets and colonial mansions adorned with swimming pools and tennis courts, Melbourne's most exclusive suburb is packed with lecherous lawyers, real estate agents and cosmetic surgeons plotting to leave their current trophy wives for the latest model, proving that while you might be able to buy a brand-new SUV, you can't buy class. A common sight in the suburb is desperate housewives, who think living inside their postcode affords them a superior status, sneering at the commoners as they drive their Toorak tractors down the rugged terrain of Toorak Road on their way to bottomless brunch with the girls.

A cradle of future prime ministers and insider traders, Toorak is the perfect place to live if you have trouble remembering whether Chardonnay is your racehorse or your mistress. The adultery capital of Victoria is actually named after the average number of breast augmentations for his mistresses the average male resident has paid for.

Recently, old mansions in Toorak have been demolished and replaced with avant-garde architectural edifices to house the nouveau riche trying to slather themselves in the reflected respectability of the welded-on upper class. Unfortunately for this bevy of tech entrepreneurs and crooked bankers, no amount of filthy lucre will ever make them inbred enough to really fit in.

Less Beverly Hills and more Vaucluse without the sea views, Toorak is where Melbourne hides its pretentious blue bloods and their well-heeled offspring so they can't bother the regular folk just trying to go about their lives.

ALSO KNOWN AS Two Rack, Spewrak, Poorak, Ew-rak.
MOST FAMOUS PEOPLE Toorak blow-ins include pretend wizard Daniel Radcliffe and pretend journalist Eddie McGuire.

St Kilda

Also known as Crap Coney Island, Shit Santa Monica or Budget Bondi, St Kilda is a trendy Melbourne beachside conclave inundated with hipsters glomming onto the suburb's 'heroin chic' reputation (which is really just heroin at this point). Anything resembling actual character has been swept aside

in a tide of gentrification, the bohemians and sex workers pushed out by the offspring of wealthy families desperately trying to live out their Bukowski fantasies. Despite featuring a beach strewn with medical waste and a main street littered with human refuse, St Kilda is still considered a desirable locale by the sort of people who call themselves 'creatives', even though they work in advertising.

St Kilda's premier attraction is Luna Park, a kitschy amusement park famous for its horrifying 'Mr Moon' sculpted face entranceway, which has contributed to the nightmares of countless children and doped-up stoners who thought it would be funny to get munted and spend all day riding the Great Scenic Railway. Another popular place is St Kilda Pier, the perfect vantage point to watch the tide wash the assorted garbage in from Port Phillip Bay. The pier is home to a colony of penguins, which makes a change from its usual disgusting denizens such as junkies, hobos and unicyclists.

St Kilda is also home to a legion of long-suffering fans of a terrible AFL team that has managed only one flag amid decades and decades of mediocrity.

ALSO KNOWN AS Shit Kilda, St Dilda.
MOST FAMOUS PEOPLE A host of artists and entertainers including famous blackface exponent Chris Lilley and *The Crocodile Hunter: Collision Course* star Magda Szubanski.

Werribee

A former country town that in recent times has become a commuter dormitory, Werribee is where Melbourne stores the riffraff that were too ratshit for Broadmeadows. It's now full of ferals who were funnelled out of gentrifying city suburbs by rising rents, resulting in horrendous traffic, soaring crime and an abundance of bogans. Werribee is Australia's capital of welfare fraud, which is so prevalent that the cops have set up stalls in shopping centres where locals can dob in a dole cheat.

A particularly dero part of Werribee is the 'Birdcage', an urban jungle that earned its name because most of its streets are named after birds. Unfortunately, during a trip down Kookaburra Crescent or Budgie Court, the only bird you

are likely to see is a Ford Falcon abandoned on a nature strip.

Werribee's visitor attractions are all crammed into Werribee Park, whose features include a mansion haunted by the ghost of the owner who topped himself due to living in Werribee, and the Werribee Open Range Zoo. Most of the zoo's animals have taken on the characteristics of true Werribeeans, which is fantastic if you want to see a giraffe that smells like shit or a hippopotamus that's really good at lodging dodgy Centrelink forms. The suburb's most famous feature is the Western Treatment Plant, a gargantuan sewage facility that deals to most of Melbourne's jobbies and gives Werribee and its inhabitants their distinctive stench. The massive poo plant means Werribee is both literally and figuratively a shit town.

TOWN SLOGAN Where I Be?
ALSO KNOWN AS Feralbee, Derobee, Terrorbee, Unbearribee.
MOST FAMOUS PEOPLE Chopper Read impersonator Merv Hughes and *Australian Idol* first loser Anthony Callea.

It wasn't always like this n most those who hanging out commercial Rd. ARE NOT EVEN FROM THIS TOWN. SO THINK YOU HAD BETTER GET YOUR FACTS RIGHT N WHAT ARE YOU ON ABOUT SALES GOT FUCKIN Dirty old COUCHES n shitty nappies n NEEDLES IN PARKS N ON FOOYPATHS MAYBE YOU SHOULD ASK THE POLITICIANS WHY THEYVE DUPED all the shit from melb down here. N maybe your soiled urself or YOUR HEADS IBVIOUSLY TOO FAR UP UR ASS YOU PROB GOT SHIT STAINED TEETH YRSELF. (Rusty Bung, Morwell)

I love Moe! whoever thought this crap up obviously hasn't lived in the town or suffers from small poppy syndrome. (Garth Pendulum, Moe)

shit comes from arsoles this moron is full of it ARSOLE (Dulloband Groobl, Frankston)

EVENT

THE MELBOURNE CUP

Australasia's pre-eminent public horse-abuse holiday, the Melbourne Cup is the only iconic sporting event where you can eat the losers. Internationally renowned as 'the race that stops a nation', the Cup has featured such famous winners as Phar Lap, Makybe Diva and a donkey on meth. Most of the horses are owned by truly objectionable people like minor royals, oil sheikhs and property developers.

Despite its pretension towards sophistication, horseracing is basically bullfights for the bourgeois, an excuse for suburbanites to dress a bit fancy and watch a midget flog half a tonne of future dog roll while losing a week's wages on a poorly constructed trifecta. The Melbourne Cup is traditionally marked with a massive orgy of public spewing and fighting, something it shares with other national holidays such as Australia Day and Russell Crowe's birthday. Post-race news coverage is dominated by footage of shit-faced tradies collapsing into hedges and ruining their best court suits, as well as half-cut slags fishing piss-soaked fascinators out of the gutter. It's the race that stops a nation's brains working.

The Big Penguin in Penguin: a tribute to the episode of *Pingu* where he experimented with disco biscuits.

CANNIBAL ALLEY

TASMANIA

SEE PAGE 116

BURNIE
PENGUIN
DEVONPORT
ULVERSTONE
LAUNCESTON
QUEENSTOWN
HOBART

ROUTE NOTES

DEVONPORT (page 118)

ULVERSTONE (page 119)

BURNIE (page 122)

QUEENSTOWN* A post-apocalyptic hellscape inhabited by all manner of mutants.

HOBART* The main tourist attraction is the Museum of Old and New Art, which is lucky because most Tasmanians can't read.

LAUNCESTON* More like 'Inceston'.

* Reviewed in *Sh*t Towns of Australia*

Devonport

Nestled in the armpit of Tasmania's northern coast is the industrial dump of Devonport. The city was formed in 1890 by the amalgamation of the cross-river towns of Turkey and Foreplay, and after covering both sides of the river mouth became known as the Herpes of the Mersey. Devonport is best known as the landing point for ferries from Melbourne and takes its name from the fact that all visitors are devastated to arrive. Most tourists bring their cars so they can drive away from Devonport as quickly as possible. Enterprising Tasmaniacs take advantage of this fact by boarding the boats in order to break into mainlanders' vehicles, scavenging for items unavailable in Tasmania such as mobile phones, laptops and toothpaste.

For anyone forced to spend time in Deroport because their car broke down between the ferry dock and the highway onramp, the city offers a range of attractions to underwhelm, including parks covered in dog shit, rocky 'beaches' covered in dog shit, and rows of empty shops on streets covered in dog shit. Arrivals by sea are greeted by a terrifying five-metre-tall statue of a typical Tasmanian male—bearded, bedraggled and naked, brandishing a pitchfork while proudly manspreading to present his metal micropenis. Nightlife in Devo centres around the local MethDonald's, the 9/11 bottle shop (which is a real thing), and the city's sole nightclub, House, which is an actual house. Other lowlights include the twelve-month winter, the complete absence of free parking, and the unavoidable resident population of inbred, toothless, chain-smoking, piss-chugging, ice-addled Karens and Darrens.

TOWN SLOGAN Devonitely a Dump!

ALSO KNOWN AS Dev, Devo, D-port, Devonhole, Deroport, Depressionport, Devonpork, Deathonport, Methonport.

Ulverstone

Ulverstone is located midway between the island's entry point of Devonport and the shithole of Burnie, making it Tasmania's taint. While no one is sure how the town got its name, it seems that, like a plethora of other Aussie shit towns, it was

likely named after a similarly punishing dump in England. The Tasmanian version has lived up to the example set by its Pommy predecessor by maintaining a 200-year unbroken streak of rampant mediocrity.

Ulverstone originally rose to prominence with loggers denuding the area in order to provide timber for the Victorian gold rush. Once the settlers were done despoiling the earth, they turned the whole thing into a giant potato farm in order to satisfy the local Irish population's insatiable spud lust.

A popular activity is taking a cruise up the River Leven, which is a great idea if you ever wanted to experience a colonoscopy from the perspective of the

FUCKING disgusting, self centred, narrow minded and IGNORANT attitude of the writer AND person posting this is worth a batch slapping!!!!! (Biff Particle, Devonport)

yes we used to be a polluted town it has all changed why don't you come down here a do you funny little jokes well not jokes just shit coming out of your mouth you funking maggot (Derek Plinth, Burnie)

What a fuck insult Lical Resudents carnt read and write Shame on you (Susan Munt, Hobart)

Get stuffed i was born inbred in Lonnie (Stacey Spool, Launceston) probe. Other popular pastimes of Ulverstoners include pub brawls, punting fairy penguins and massive amounts of incest.

One of Ulverstone's premier attractions is the Gunns Plains Caves, a vast network of underground caverns that were allegedly discovered when a possum fell through a hole in the ground (or at least that's what the guy who was trying to do God-knows-what to a possum told everyone). After spending any length of time in Ulverstone, dying a suffocating death somewhere dark and claustrophobic might seem like a good idea.

TOWN SLOGAN Who'd Leven Ulverstone?
ALSO KNOWN AS Ulvie, Ulverrock, Hole-verstone, Liverstone, Vulvastone, Incestone.

Burnie ☢ ☺ ✕

Once home to a paper mill, a paint factory and an acid plant, Burnie was for many years Australia's most polluted city, famous for its obnoxious odour and stained red sea. In fact, it was such a polluted hellhole that it inspired a Midnight Oil song, putting it in such illustrious company as the asbestos wasteland of Wittenoom and the nuclear nightmare of Maralinga. Fortunately, Burnie's belching plants have since closed, taking with them the majority of the town's jobs. Nevertheless, Burnie lingers like that stubborn nugget that refuses to flush and remains a major exporter of woodchips and bogans.

One of Burnie's greatest achievements was somehow tricking cruise ships into docking there for the most disappointing stop of their tour. In Burnie it rains for approximately 26 hours per day and is so cold that thousands of sheep imported by settlers in the 1820s promptly froze to death. Local sights are limited to an unsightly port, the world's biggest woodchip pile and a boring boardwalk along a rugged, penguin-infested coast. Strangely, it is impossible to find a parking space in Burnie even though all of the shops are boarded up.

There is no nightlife or normal entertainment in Burnie—as locals will tell you, the only thing to do there is your cousin. Residents thus resort to the traditional Tasmanian pastimes of incest, cannibalism and hooning ('Burnie' is short for 'Place to do Burnouts'). Burnians are also known for their rampant homophobia—if you want to root a relative, you'd better make damn sure they're a different gender.

TOWN SLOGAN Burnie, Not Worth the Journey!
ALSO KNOWN AS Bleurghnie, Boganie, Bumhole.
DID YOU KNOW? Burnie hosts an annual event called 'Weekend at Burnie', in which locals dress up and display their taxidermied grandparents.

TOP 25
SHIT TOWN SONGS

We've got your Aussie road trip soundtrack covered with this playlist of famous songs about Australia's shit towns.

1. 6ix9ine—'Yeppoonani'
2. AC/DC—'It's Geelong Way to the Top (If You Wanna Rock 'n' Roll)'
3. The Association—'Along Comes Maryborough'
4. The Beatles—'Albury Fields Forever'
5. The Beatles—'Adelaidy Madonna'
6. Bill Haley & His Comets—'Rockhampton Around the Clockhampton'
7. Daft Punk—'One Moree Time'
8. Dire Straits—'Brothers in Armidale'
9. Bob Dylan—'Cessnockin' on Heaven's Door'
10. Green Day—'Boulevard of Broken Hill'
11. Elton John—'Rocket Mandurah'

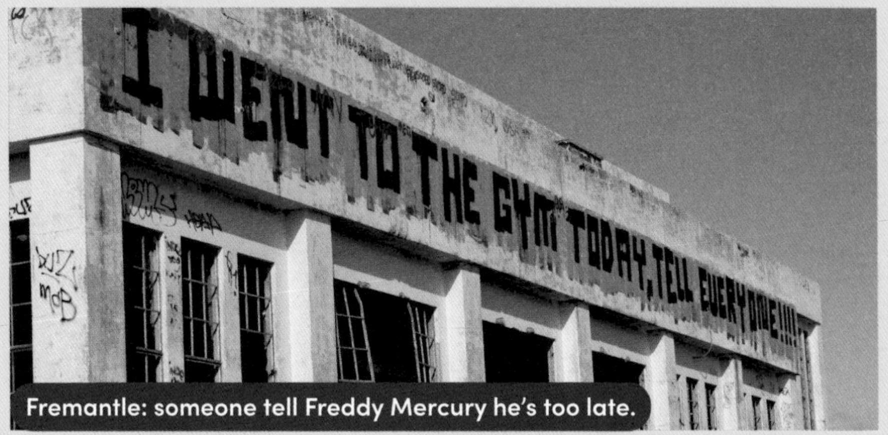

Fremantle: someone tell Freddy Mercury he's too late.

12. Tom Jones—'What's New, Pussykatoomba?'
13. Metallica—'For Whom the Ballarat Tolls'
14. Metallica—'Wherever I May Roma'
15. Mark Morrison—'Return of the Mackay'
16. Johnny Nash—'I Kempsey Clearly Now'
17. The Notorious B.I.G.—'Moe Money Moe Problems'
18. Queen—'I Want to Break Fremantle'
19. The Rolling Stones—'Wild Horshams'
20. The Sex Pistols—'God Save the Queanbeyan'
21. Simon and Garfunkel—'Murray Bridge Over Troubled Water'
22. Frank Sinatra—'Newcastle, Newcastle'
23. Will Smith—'Just the Toowoomba'
24. Soundgarden—'Pretty Noosa'
25. Britney Spears—'Hit Me Baby Lismore Time'

The Lovecraftian atrocity known as the Big Lobster, Kingston SE.

THE DEVIL'S GOOCH

MELBOURNE TO ADELAIDE

MILDURA
ADELAIDE
MURRAY BRIDGE
HORSHAM
BENDIGO
KINGSTON SE
ARARAT
BALLARAT
MOUNT GAMBIER
MELBOURNE
GEELONG
WARRNAMBOOL
TWELVE APOSTLES

ROUTE NOTES

COASTAL ROUTE

GEELONG* An open-air bogan sanctuary.

TWELVE APOSTLES Seven (formerly eight) big rocks in the sea. The most famous feature of the 'Great Ocean Road' (and proof that Victorians can't count).

WARRNAMBOOL (page 130)

MOUNT GAMBIER* Known for its pillars of limestone and mountains of meth.

MURRAY BRIDGE (page 134)

ADELAIDE* The City of Churches, Pubs and Serial Killers (see Elizabeth, page 138).

INLAND ROUTE

OPTIONAL DETOUR: BENDIGO* Once a ramshackle shanty town for grubby miners, now a ramshackle city for grubby housos.

BALLARAT* See Bendigo.

ARARAT (page 131)

HORSHAM (page 133)

OPTIONAL DETOUR: MILDURA* Features roads named after its main industries including Orange Street, Lemon Street and Insurance Fraud Avenue.

* Reviewed in *Sh*t Towns of Australia*

Warrnambool

Situated at the wrong end of the Great Ocean Road on Victoria's summerless southern coast, Warrnambool is a wind-blasted crater where the cloud never clears and it's always too cold to swim. The unspellable joint's best attempt at a point of interest is the Mahogany Ship, the reputed wreck of a Portuguese caravel supposedly buried in the sands of Armstrong Bay. Despite no actual evidence of such a relic, residents have perpetuated the myth largely because it's the only vaguely interesting thing that has ever allegedly happened there. The Victorian government once offered a $250,000 reward to anyone who could produce evidence of the Mahogany Ship, but alas the elusive vessel has proven harder to find than Harold Holt.

Warrnambool's only other claim to fame—apart from making a great Scrabble score—is being the shooting location for the infamous Tom Selleck stinker *Quigley Down Under*. The box office flop was so horrendous that its only lasting legacy was the unusual number of moustachioed babies born in the

Bool roughly nine months after filming wrapped.

Aside from entertaining fantasies of buried boats, the most popular activity in Warrnambool is participating in the 'gap challenge', in which bored locals try to stuff themselves through a 30-centimetre slit between two buildings on Timor Street. Given the girth of the average Warrnamboolian, local emergency services are kept very busy.

The most famous landmarks in town are the Dirty Angel—a statue of a heavenly creature having a cheeky wank—and the Silver Ball, a scrotesque structure that hovers over town like a ratshit UFO. Locals know that once they see the Silver Ball they've made it back to Warrnambool, a realisation that probably makes them wish they had been abducted by aliens.

ALSO KNOWN AS Warnie, the Bool, Warrnamboring, Warmmyballs, Wornouthole, Warrnambowel.
MOST FAMOUS PERSON Oddball, the first dog to win the Grand Annual Steeplechase.
DID YOU KNOW? Warrnambool was named after cricketer Shane Warne.

Ararat

Originally a gold rush town, Ararat has reinvented itself as a thriving dumping ground for the socially unacceptable. There are three types of people there: fatties, perverts and nutjobs—although these groups are by no means mutually exclusive.

The main reason 'Ararat' was chosen as the town's name is that it's the easiest word to pronounce with a mouth full of KFC. Araratbags' reputation

as gluttonous chubsters is so renowned that the producers of *The Biggest Loser* wisely chose to film there in 2014. It's no wonder the salad-dodger city is widely known as Arafat.

Ararat is also inextricably linked with wankers, diddlers and other sex pests. In a remarkable display of foresight by its founders, the town's name can be typed using only the left hand, which is handy as people from Ararat are invariably using their right one to furiously masturbate whenever they are anywhere near a computer. Analrat even hosts Victoria's premier paedo prison, the Hopkins Erectional Correctional Centre.

'Ararat' also happens to sound like someone with a brain injury trying to say 'Ballarat', which is apt as it's also famous for its mental health facilities. The city formerly hosted the Aradale Mental Hospital and J Ward, a 'lunatic asylum for the criminally insane'. Both institutions closed in the 1990s, with their inmates released to blend seamlessly into the local community. Incredibly, Aradale was the site of a reported 13,000 deaths in its 130-year history. It is now used for ghost tours, with common reports of visitors fainting, feelings of nausea and disturbing smells, although these complaints are also common among visitors to anywhere in Ararat.

ALSO KNOWN AS The Rathole, Rat Vegas, Arafat, Analrat, Aracrap, Arsehat.

Horsham

Horsham's greatest cultural contribution is the 'florrie', a flat, crumbed piece of horse steak wrapped around a slice of ham and a bit of cheese. This innovative combination of horse and ham is actually how Horsham got its name. Coincidentally, Horsham is also Old English for 'whores' home', an unkind yet not entirely inaccurate label.

Aside from florries and dicks, Horshamites' favourite thing to shove in their gobs is crack pipes. In fact, the city's Second Amendment guarantees all of its citizens the right to carry a crystal pistol at all times. The only people in Horsham not munted on meth are those who are both underage and pregnant, who take it easy by sticking to binge drinking.

Horsham is a hub of intellectual pursuits like gossip, bigotry and fighting with baseball bats. Its most educated residents are young women with diplomas in hairdressing, who harbour lofty dreams of moving to somewhere fancier like Shepparton and making it on OnlyFans. These ambitious overachievers are the exception, however—most Horshamers are just happy if their welfare cheque covers their ice bill.

The town was once visited by literary icon Mark Twain, who was left with an abiding impression of its overwhelming flatness. Unfortunately, Twain wasn't referring to the terrain but rather the locals' pronounced lack of cleavage—Horsham is notorious for its flat-chested floozies (which sadly has a serious impact on those aforementioned OnlyFans dreams).

Nearby Dadswells Bridge is home to the Giant Koala, a gigantic red-eyed, hairy-eared replica of the only creature with more chlamydia than a local youth. The Giant Koala is the perfect mascot for the area: awkward, disfigured and looking like it's been up for three days straight on a JobSeeker-funded meth binge.

ALSO KNOWN AS Sham, Whoresham, Horshame, Horseshit.

MOST FAMOUS PERSON Actress Portia de Rossi, who preferred to move to America and marry the meanest woman alive rather than stay for another second in Horsham.

DID YOU KNOW? The Giant Koala is worshipped as a god by the primitive Horsham townsfolk.

Murray Bridge

Most shit towns derive their names from a colourful bit of local lore or a notorious character. Murray Bridge, on

The world's only gift shop housed in a marsupial's vagina.

the other hand, is so named because it has a bridge over the Murray River, earning it a brutally banal name that sounds more like a local councillor convicted on sex tourism charges than a bland riverside hamlet. The only way the town could have a less imaginative moniker is if it were renamed Methface McCentrelink. Little wonder then that Murray Bridge is burdened by a barrage of nicknames, from the Boganese Muzza Bizza to Murray Fridge, an allusion to all the ice.

The most popular attraction in Murray Bridge is the Bunyip, a grotesque, screaming mechanical monster and local deity entrapped in a cage of stagnant pond water that visitors pay to see, smell and scare the shit out of their children. The Bunyip was originally created as a cruel and unusual punishment for the town's numerous juvenile delinquents, but like most things in Murray Bridge, those same delinquents turned the punishment into a perverse sexual rite of passage. Local youths often sport tattoos commemorating their attempts at 'riding the Bunyip'.

It's a little-known fact that Murray Bridge was a former residence of Snowtown psychopath John Bunting. While butchering people, Bunting enjoyed playing the Live album *Throwing Copper*, a record that appropriately includes the song 'Shit Towne'. It's unclear whether being mutilated and stuffed into a barrel or being forced to listen to 'I Alone' is a bigger crime.

When it isn't inspiring serial killers, Murray Bridge is also home to a round of the Australian International Paedo Prix, in which a field of sex offenders compete to see who can abduct a child

The information on eureka is totally inaccurate this anoys me to no end which of you milenial snoflakes wrote this dribble. **(Tony Jabroni, Ballarat)**

Shit town Australia wouldn't know shit from clay ,Horsham is a great town .and the floozies have big titties **(Steve Chubb, Horsham)**

Must be an immigrant writhing this
(Khe Sahn Underarm, Adelaide)

from a playground in the shortest possible time. Other popular activities in Murray Bridge include smoking the 'bogan saxophone', joining a bikie gang, getting into a fight in an IGA car park, or staring into the empty riverbed where the Murray used to flow.

ALSO KNOWN AS Muzza Bizza, Mullet Bridge, Methy Bridge, Murray Fridge, Durry Bridge, Slurry Bridge.

Elizabeth

A planned satellite slum in the far northern reaches of Adelaide, Elizabeth is essentially Adelaide's Logan, Penrith or Werribee. Due to a restraining order taken out by Adelaide, Elizabeth must stay at least 25 kilometres from the CBD at all times.

Despite being swallowed by the new City of Playford in 1997, the former city of Elizabeth—now a loose conurbation of suburbs—maintains a cultural distinction based on a proud tradition of unfiltered antisocial boganness. Suburbs considered part of the informal Elizabeth area include Elizabeth, Elizabeth North, Elizabeth East, Elizabeth South, not Elizabeth West, Elizabeth Downs, Elizabeth Grove, Elizabeth Park, Elizabeth Vale, Elizabeth Taylor, Elizabeth Smart, Queen Elizabeth II and Elizabeth Báthory.

Elizabeth is Australia's version of Detroit in that it's known for an automobile manufacturing industry that no longer exists (uness you count body shops respraying stolen cars), and like Detroit it is now a desolate wasteland with a 100 per cent unemployment rate. The entire Elizabeth area is dotted with abandoned overgrown lots covered with car corpses, mattresses and old couches, which are surrounded by blocks of decaying units and thriving meth labs.

Without gainful employment to distract them, 'Lizbeff' locals are free to devote themselves to hobbies such as drinking, drugs, fighting in the street, beating up bus drivers, stabbing people on the train, ransacking construction sites, stealing the wheels off cars, stealing cars off their wheels, robbing people's houses while they're out, and robbing people's houses while they're home. If you aren't being assaulted by a dole bludger, choking on burnout fumes or wading through a torrent of used syringes, you're probably squeezing past the Holden SS ute that has ploughed into your living room.

It's no mean feat to be the worst part of Adelaide, a city famous for serial killers and paedophiles, but Elizabeth has nailed it.

ALSO KNOWN AS Lizzy, Lizbeff, The Biff, Elizameth.
MOST FAMOUS PERSON Jimmy Barnes, budget Springsteen and Australia's most prolific provider of pub brawl soundtracks.

TOP 10 DUMBEST REGIONAL FOODS

Australians are famously adventurous and equally famously feral, so it's no surprise that they eat some truly disgusting dishes. By way of warning, here are some of the weirdest, dumbest and rankest regional foods you are likely to encounter on an Aussie road trip.

1. **PIE FLOATER (ADELAIDE)** A meat pie dumped upside down in a bowl of pea soup and topped with tomato sauce, the pie floater was almost certainly invented by accident. Why anyone would want to repeat that culinary disaster is anyone's guess.
2. **SMILEY FRITZ (ADELAIDE)** A variation of bung fritz (anus sausage) with marks resembling facial features, slices of smiley fritz are traditionally given to children in South Australian supermarkets so they can bite eye holes and wear them as a mask. Ideal for any budding Ed Gein.
3. **BALFOURS FROG CAKE (ADELAIDE)** Sponge, cream and fondant sculpted into the shape of a frog's head, this is the perfect dessert for people who want to pretend they're Ozzy Osbourning an amphibian.
4. **CHEESE SLAW (BROKEN HILL)** An unholy melange of cheddar, carrot and emu semen that only the truly depraved would claim is food.

5. **CHEESE AND CARROT SALAD (PORT PIRIE)** Port Pirie's shit answer to cheese slaw.
6. **RATBAIT (PORT PIRIE)** Cheese and bacon baked on bread. It's called ratbait because you'd have to be vermin to eat that shit.
7. **CHIKO ROLL (NATIONWIDE)** Invented in Bendigo and unveiled in Wagga Wagga, the Chiko Roll has spread like nits in Nimbin to become a supposed Australian icon—despite being owned by an American company and being basically the same thing as a Chinese spring roll. 'Chiko' is short for 'chicken', even though they don't contain any. A more accurate name would be 'Cabbage Roll' or 'Calorie Tube'.
8. **DIM SIM (MELBOURNE/ NATIONWIDE)** Originating in Melbourne's Chinatown but now a takeaway staple across Australia, the giant dumpling known as a dim sim or 'dimmy' is great if you're craving a meal that resembles a boiled ballsack.
9. **FLORRIE (HORSHAM)** A flat, crumbed piece of horse steak wrapped around a slice of ham and a bit of cheese, often drowned in gravy to mask the awful taste.
10. **BIN CHICKEN PARMI (LOGAN)** Logan put its own twist on an Aussie pub grub classic by substituting chicken for the much cheaper ibis. Consisting of breaded bin chicken breast smothered in tomato sauce and grilled parmesan and served with chips, this local delicacy makes Logan the ideal place for intrepid tourists to try some disease-riddled tip turkey.

The Big Stubby, Larrimah: an enduring monument to locals' commitment to problem drinking.

FALCONIO DRIVE

ADELAIDE TO DARWIN

SEE PAGE 144

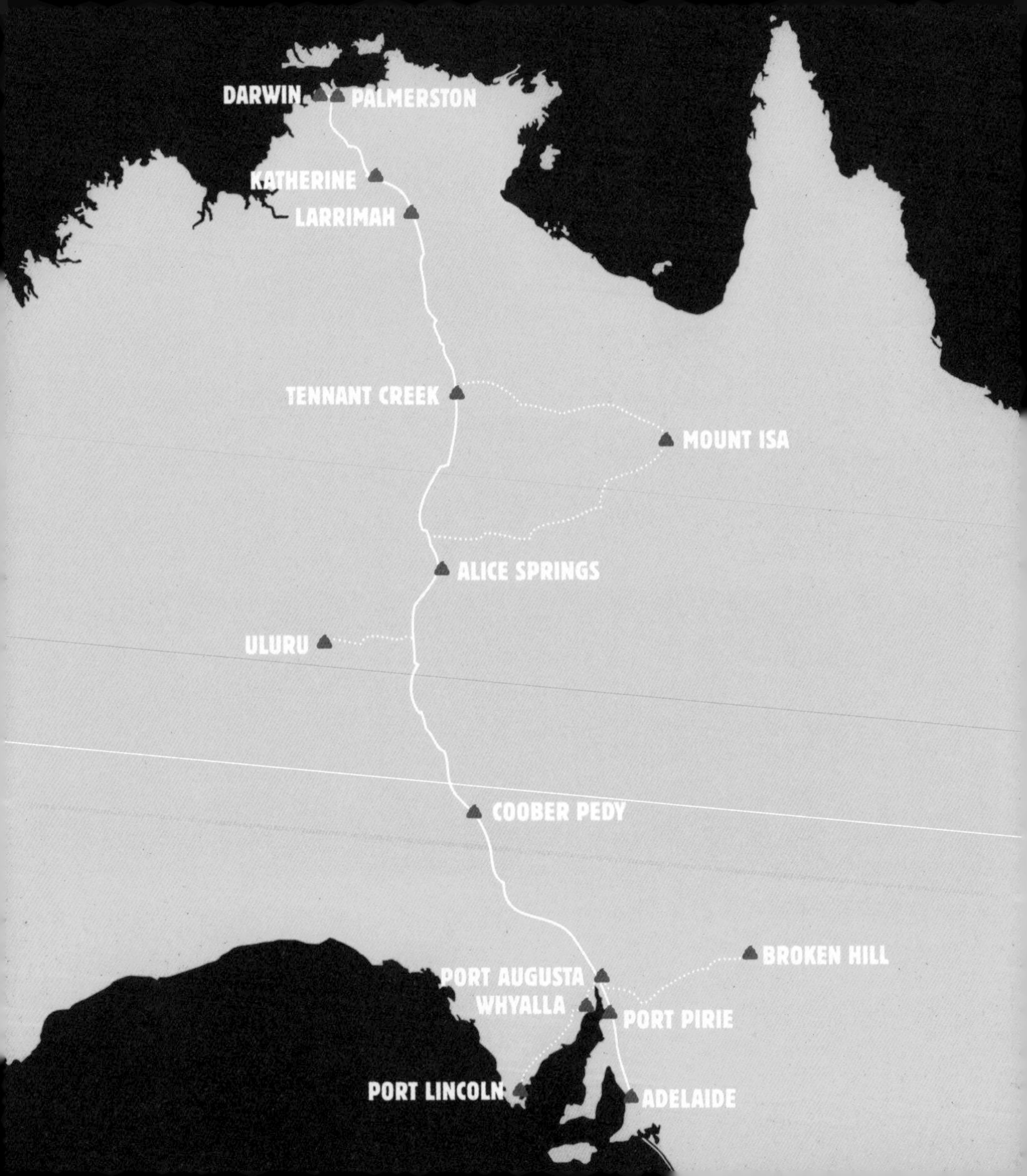

DARWIN
PALMERSTON
KATHERINE
LARRIMAH
TENNANT CREEK
MOUNT ISA
ALICE SPRINGS
ULURU
COOBER PEDY
BROKEN HILL
PORT AUGUSTA
WHYALLA
PORT PIRIE
PORT LINCOLN
ADELAIDE

ROUTE NOTES

PORT PIRIE* Proof that you don't need hills to have hillbillies.

PORT AUGUSTA* Where the dirt meets the sea.

OPTIONAL DETOUR: BROKEN HILL* Basically an inhabited slag heap.

OPTIONAL DETOUR: WHYALLA (page 146) and **PORT LINCOLN** (page 148)

COOBER PEDY* A dystopian wasteland where leathery opal noodlers live like moles in subterranean bunkers.

OPTIONAL DETOUR: ULURU Or 'Ayers Rock' in Racist Old White Person.

ALICE SPRINGS* Australia's geographic anus and world stabbing capital.

OPTIONAL DETOUR: MOUNT ISA* If you're here, you're lost.

TENNANT CREEK (page 150)

KATHERINE* What Tennant Creek wants to be when it grows up.

PALMERSTON (page 152)

DARWIN* A live-action replica of what could be expected to happen to a major Australian city in a nuclear apocalypse.

* Reviewed in *Sh*t Towns of Australia*

Whyalla

Known as Steal City due to locals' propensity for nicking anything that isn't nailed down, Whyalla was originally christened Hummock Hill, meaning 'Hill Hill'. It was later renamed Whyalla, which means 'I don't know' in a local Indigenous language, or 'shithole' in English.

Whyalla is also known as Brown Town, though a more accurate name would be 'Orange Hole' due to the entire place being coated in several layers of powder the colour of Pauline Hanson's pubes. Spewed from the city's struggling steelworks, the omnipresent orange dust has been blamed for Whyalla's soaring lung cancer rates, though the local practice of chain-smoking gutter butts can't help either.

Located on the untamed Eyre Peninsula, Whyalla manages

the neat trick of being a hot, dry, dusty desert dump despite being right on the sea. Replete with plague-like populations of flies and the pervasive stench of saltbush, the area is not only an actual desert but also a cultural desert, where fine dining is chips and gravy and entertainment consists of getting fingered behind the Foodland after downing a warm goon sack.

Once an industrial hub, a slew of closures have rendered Whyalla a Centrelink mecca servicing a bounty of braindead bogans and more hordes of shambling ferals than the average episode of *The Walking Dead*. As well as being Disneyland for dole bludgers, Whyalla is also the single mother capital of South Australia, which is quite an achievement considering the state of the city's females.

Aside from getting parro

or preggo, popular pastimes include doing burnouts around roundabouts, waiting outside Coles on dole day to rush in and buy some durries and iced coffee, or crapping on a barbecue at a caravan park. A fun day out is 'chucking a beachy', which consists of drink-driving a hotwired Holden to the beach while blasting terrible music at full volume and yelling sexual propositions out the window at underage girls, before circling the car park and driving home.

TOWN SLOGAN Whyalla—Why Bother?
ALSO KNOWN AS Steel City, Brown Town, Yalla, Pig City, Whyami, Whyanus.
DID YOU KNOW? Whyalla is the sole producer of rail and steel sleepers in Australia, which are also the local weapon of choice.

Port Lincoln

Named by Matthew Flinders after his favourite nu-metal band Linkin Park, Port Lincoln only exists so people can confuse it with Port Augusta and Port Pirie. Port Lincoln is the one with less lead poisoning and more tuna—the Eyre Peninsula's fishy foreskin. Stinkin' Lincoln is so tuna-focused that it holds an annual tuna festival featuring a tuna-throwing contest, offers bored tourists the chance to swim with caged tuna, and even elected a tuna mayor. It also hunts the shit out of critically endangered bluefin tuna and invented the ecologically disastrous tuna ranching practice, proving that it's not so much the fish that the town celebrates but the obscene amounts of cash it brings in.

Once poverty-stricken, Port Lincoln has been transformed

I'm still not seeing the humour in these posts I'm old I have read funny posts before and witnessed funny things but at the moment this is not funny you should change your name to shit posts of Australia or better still just stop posting this sort of crap **(Myrtle Rust, Whyalla)**

Who is the faaarrrk wit??Im betting he's sitting in his parents home in mummies dressing gown fully lubed up getting his jollies of. Love to see the little tosser turn up to the town after mentioning this, he'd end up at a dental clinic wondering why the world is RUFF. Was a great town to grow up in&great joint to go back and visit and on many occasions I wish I could still live there. But I guess he's being funny huh?? What'd be funnier is watching this clown eating a corn on the cob with NO FKN TEETH **(Jamie Clunge, Whyalla)**

don't come back then you vaginal discharge **(Lloyd Floyd, Whyalla)** by tuna money and now boasts the most millionaires per capita in Australia—i.e. cashed-up fisherbogans living a beer lifestyle on a champagne budget. A short wander from the water reveals that the salmon-pink mansions and fancy new shops are a mere facade and, despite the tarting up, Port Lincoln is still quite the shithole—basically Whyalla with a bad Bangkok facelift. The sea and scenery are ruined by tuna farms and the shithouse beaches are covered in rubbish from fishing fleets. The local reservoir is no longer drinkable due to pollution and salinity. There is nothing for residents to do short of crashing a stolen jet ski into a fishing boat. This town proves that money can't buy class—although it can buy ice. Clearly, Port Lincoln has taken to heart that old adage: let bogans be bogans.

ALSO KNOWN AS PL, Tuna Town, Stinkin' Lincoln, Port Linkin.
MOST FAMOUS PERSON Makybe Diva, horse.

Tennant Creek

'Blessed are those who see beauty in all things, for they have never been to Tennant Creek.'—Jesus, probably

No trip to the Northern Territory is complete without taking in the outback outhouse called Tennant Creek. Conveniently located in the middle of fucking nowhere, the town is popular with everyone from disaster tourists to senile grey nomads, as well as backpackers who are intent on disappearing without a trace.

Accommodation options are plentiful: from campgrounds with twelve-foot razor wire–tipped

walls, to concrete motel rooms with barred windows, you can tailor your stay based on your own personal prison preference!

The experience doesn't end there, as any adventure outside of your rented cell will immediately immerse you in the colourful atmosphere of Tennant Creek, which usually involves witnessing a resident defecating in the middle of the road before you are shanked by a solvent-sniffing sex offender. If you're lucky, you may even be invited to a fight by a child with measles and a makeshift weapon. When conversing with a local, be sure to refer to them by the affectionate demonym 'BITCH', an acronym for 'Born In Tennant Creek Hospital'.

Tennant Creek is known for its long and proud history of

alcoholism, stretching back to the time it was founded when a truck carrying beer broke down and people set up a camp around it. Don't miss a visit to a local bottle shop, where it is traditional to queue up all morning until the industrial-strength roller doors creak open at 4 p.m.

The town is also famous for its spectacular scenery, which includes world-class examples of rock formations, car wrecks and rusting cyclone fences. If a friendly local offers to show you the Devils Marbles, Nobles Nob or The Shaft, don't worry—he's not about to flop out his genitals but is offering to take you to see a bunch of boring boulders, a big hole in the ground and a closed nightclub. The most popular local event is a rodeo, where residents take a break from abusing each other to abuse some animals.

ALSO KNOWN AS Tetanus Creek, Tennant Creep, Tennant Crack, TFC, Wolf Creek.

Palmerston

Built in the 1980s to house Darwin's rejects and saddled with the city's unwanted old name, Palmerston is the epitome of sloppy seconds. The planned satellite city is filled with people driven out of Darwin by rising house prices, which makes a nice change from people being driven out of Darwin by people who live in Palmerston. Despite a climate so inhospitable that the air is easier to drink than breathe, Palmerslum is inhabited by numerous dangerous lifeforms including crocs, river snakes and gangs of grog-guzzling gronks.

Palmerstonians are creatures of habit, engaging in several regular traditions. On 'Thirsty

Know all fuck alls talking about places most have never been need to get out and about more there's much worse places around and apart for seriously bad juvenile crime rate pt Lincoln is a great community and a good place to raise a family. And the dudes talking about the tuna industry go back to my opening line know all fuck alls. Poor bastards! **(Winky Portcullis, Port Lincoln)**

stair the towns and people you run down in the face and say your peice see if you have the back bone to do it **(Johnny Nachos, Port Lincoln)**

We aren't bothering to comment/defend because this is so far fetched and pathetic, it's not worth our time or effort! **(Max Wank, Port Augusta)**

Thursdays' they celebrate dole day by redistributing their payments to the local bottle-o. On Friday, Saturday, Sunday, Monday, Tuesday and Wednesday mornings, they patiently wait outside the police station for their loved ones to be released from the drunk tank. Once a week, Palmerstoners cut another couple of inches off their neighbour's hose to make a new bottle bong. And every night they hold fun family events that normally involve drink-driving their unmuffled shitboxes to brand-new housing developments, where they decorate the freshly laid roads with vast murals of skid marks. Other popular Palmerston pastimes include punching grey nomads, pissing on passed-out long grassers, and tipping recent hospital patients out of their wheelchairs to pinch their catheter bags after mistaking them for goon.

ALSO KNOWN AS Palmerslum, Darwin's Dunny.

Key board warriors again . Go get a life an piss of under the rock ya come from or better ! ya bubble .Its people like you drag this town down. Us who lived here seen all come an go for better or worse . As with all towns around Australia . So if you dont like it get on ya high horse an go to another place to run down . (Keith Smithticles, Port Augusta)

More lick the cock drop spent 2hours here in the eighties, I'll bet (Bart Shart, Tennant Creek)

Terrible that this type of rubbish is being peddles around. Creator has his head up his own oriphus. (Wayne Shorn, Palmerston)

TOP 25 SHIT TOWN MOVIES

Get in the Aussie road trip spirit with these classic films about Australia's shit towns.

1. *Adelaidy and the Tramp*
2. *Alice Springs in Wonderland*
3. *Apocalypse Nowra*
4. *Ballaratatouille*
5. *Bedknobs and Broomesticks*
6. *Bendigo Like Beckham*
7. *Brokeback Mount Isa*
8. *The Broken Hills Have Eyes*
9. *Dubbo Jeopardy*
10. *Geelongest Yard*
11. *The Good Shepparton*
12. *Goulburn After Reading*
13. *Harold and Kumar Go to Newcastle*
14. *Harry Potter and the Philosopher's Gladstone*
15. *Journey to the Centre of the Perth*
16. *The Lion Kingaroy*
17. *Maitland of the Dead*
18. *Mandela: Long Walk to Fremantle*
19. *MelBourne Identity*
20. *Murray Bridge to Terabithia*
21. *School of Rockhampton*
22. *Seal Team Six: The Raid on Nimbin Laden*
23. *Supermandurah*
24. *There's Something About Maryborough*
25. *Logan*

A heavily made-up Jack Black on the set of *School of Rockhampton.*

The Big Boxing Croc, Humpty Doo: a memorial to the only pugilist in Australia with less credibility than Paul Gallen.

METHAMPHETAMINE HIGHWAY

DARWIN TO PERTH

SEE PAGE 160

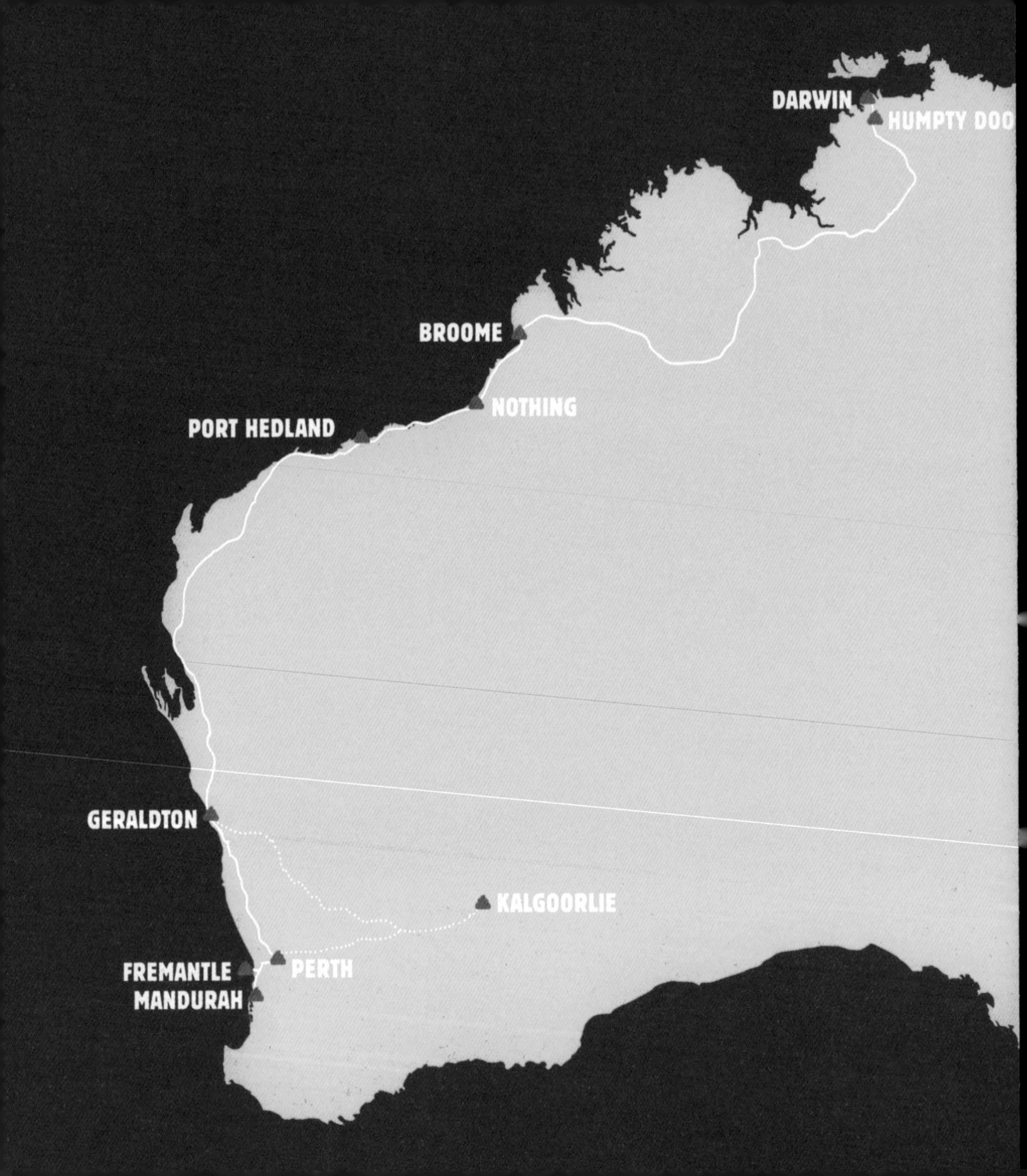

DARWIN
HUMPTY DOO
BROOME
NOTHING
PORT HEDLAND
GERALDTON
KALGOORLIE
FREMANTLE
PERTH
MANDURAH

ROUTE NOTES

BROOME* The Gateway to Nowhere.

PORT HEDLAND (page 162)

GERALDTON (page 164)

OPTIONAL DETOUR: KALGOORLIE* Founded by criminals and prostitutes who had been cast out of polite society, essentially making it Australia's Australia.

PERTH* One of the most isolated capital cities in the world, fortunately for everyone else (pages 165–169).

FREMANTLE* Where WA keeps its hipsters and 'boho bogans'.

MANDURAH* Junkies and geriatrics.

* Reviewed in *Sh*t Towns of Australia*

Port Hedland

Situated in north-west Who Cares, Port Hedland is a derelict minerals discharge hole dressed up as a town. The iron anus owes its name to its turd-brown eyesore of a port, the proliferation of substance enthusiasts offering 'head' on its streets, and its inhabitants' inability to spell. Isolated, full of flies and ferals and hot as all buggery, the prospect of living in the Pilbara poo pit is about as enticing as a proposition from Gina Rinehart.

Port Hedland promotes itself as the sunniest place in Australia, a dubious honour that's a bit like claiming to be the coldest village in the Arctic or the most incestuous town in Tasmania. Cattle and sheep farming was once a major industry for the town, but this ended when the animals all withered to a crisp. The only fauna able to survive Port Deadland's intense heat are creatures like red-necked stints, red-necked avocets and red-necked people. The town is also home to the Australian bustard and plenty of Australian bastards.

Port Hedland's main industries are shitting out iron ore, digging holes and dole bludging. Popular pastimes include racing wheelbarrows, smashing people's solar panels and being hospitalised with a respiratory infection caused by iron ore dust. The town hosted a beachfront boat-people prison from 1991 to 2004 that is now a hotel—the number of people staying has significantly dropped since the locks were removed.

Saddled with enough shitness to fill the Big Wheelbarrow itself, Port Hedland has resorted to desperate measures to downplay

Australia is famous for its breathtaking vistas and natural beauty.

its reputation: by surrounding itself with a splattering of even shittier settlements like South Hedland, Marble Bar and Karratha.

TOWN SLOGAN Wipe Your Feet on the Way Out!
DID YOU KNOW? Port Hedland's Pier Hotel reportedly holds the world record for the most stabbings recorded in a single night.

Geraldton

Geraldton is called Geraldton because everyone there is called Gerald. Types of Geralds include barefoot bogan Geralds who brawl on the beach, feral Geralds who steal ciggie butts off people's front porches, boatie Geralds who import ice while pretending to catch crayfish, snobby Geralds who get stiffies from the rising price of their rapidly eroding beachfront properties, and already numerous 'Kmart mum' Geraldines, even though the town only got a Kmart in 2021.

All of these Geralds are crammed into an isolated redneck town somewhere on the desolate west coast, renowned for its relentless howling wind that sounds like a horror movie soundtrack. The city is also famous for its white sand beaches—what the brochures don't mention is that they are covered in huge piles of rotting seaweed, making the entire town smell like an open sewer. Popular tourist activities include sandboarding (throwing yourself down a dune and getting sand in every orifice before slogging back up again) and water sports (getting blown out to sea on a kiteboard and eaten by a shark).

Geraldton's premier visitor attraction is the wreck of the

Batavia, an old ship crewed by a bunch of Dutch maniacs who lost their shit and massacred each other after realising they had crash-landed at Geraldton. On dry land, the best Dero Gero can offer is a melted airport runway and the Leaning Trees of Greenough, two features that serve as permanent reminders of the area's punishing weather.

ALSO KNOWN AS Gerald, Dero Gero, Feralton.
MOST FAMOUS PERSON Bradley John Murdoch, extreme anti-tourism protester.

Armadale

Originally built around a pub and named after a vodka brand, the alcoholic country town of Armadale has in recent decades been swallowed by urban sprawl to become an outer suburb of Perth. Consequently, its population is a mash-up of inbred country bumpkins and drug-addled urban deros, who have crossbred to create a truly terrifying subspecies of bogan. The suburb's slogan is 'City Living, Country Style', which is a polite way of saying the inmates are adept at smoking meth with their webbed fingers.

Armadale's streets are adorned with piles of broken booze bottles, rows of burnt-out cars and towers of shopping trolleys. Shops and bars usually sport signs imploring customers to don footwear, as most locals tend to get around barefoot due to the difficulty of finding thongs that fit six-toed feet. The area has recently become inundated with first home buyers, as there is a surfeit of houses available at a great price because people were murdered in them. After moving in, new Armadillos quickly find themselves praying for a civilising wave of gentrification or a tactical nuclear weapon blast, whichever comes first.

Armadale's most famous feature is the Old Jarrah Tree, an 800-year-old eucalyptus in a car park that has survived numerous attempts at ringbarking by local residents, who are jealous that the tree is the smartest inhabitant of Armadale. Another popular attraction is Pioneer World, where locals can see the historical conditions that their convict forebears endured and hope that they too might commit a crime heinous enough to see them deported to the other side of the world. Armadale is also home to Cole's Shaft, which he will be more than happy to show you

Who Eva rote this shit need to be shot my the japs this me town & you lot don't know wat ur takling about **(Dusty Molasses, Darwin)**

The writter of this shit is a fcktards arsehole
If you don't like it here the feeling is mutual
We hate your very being **(Peter Emery, Darwin)**

NOT ALL Broome peoples aren't as rotten like what's been posted. so go and poke your Holes **(Stan Mangina, Broome)**

What a cunt of a man or woman that wrote us up with such glamour penach an CLASS how fukn dare you may your ears turn in to arseholes an shit all over your persona... **(Girt Substance, Port Hedland)**

How does go get fu$&ed sound tunts
(Florence Funnel, Kalgoorlie)

around the back of Bunnings if you ask him nicely.

TOWN SLOGAN Shitty Living, Bumpkin Style.
ALSO KNOWN AS Armahole, Dramadale, Farmadale, Amishdale, Armafail, Armajail, Scumidale, Armadump, Armpit, Armadildo.

Rockingham

Named after its official currency, crack rock, Rockingham is a failed port turned poor man's tourist town. Visitors flock to Rocko from all over the Perth metropolitan area to pester a pelican or fondle a dolphin, offload their unwanted elderly to one of the numerous nursing homes, have a seaside street fight or shoot up on some sand. One of the city's main strands is Palm Beach, which sits on Cockburn Sound—interestingly, both names were inspired by a particularly furious masturbation session by coloniser Thomas Peel. With incessant gales, nearby Safety Bay is ideal for windsurfing, kitesurfing and, ironically, drowning.

Rockingham first became a desirable daytrip destination for Perthlings in the early twentieth century as it was within driving distance of the state crapital, but far enough away that the Pertherts could legally binge on booze on Sundays during an era when sales were strictly prohibited in their own city for dumb religious reasons, before drink-driving the 50 kilometres home again. To this day, chugging cheap piss until you pass out remains Rockingham's official sport. Other popular pub games include punching on with a navy jock in knock-off sunnies, getting glassed by a FIFO fuckwit with a

neck tatt and rat's tail, or having a hoon on a welfare daddy–seeking single mum.

Aside from its abundance of boofheads, Rockingham is most famous for the *Catalpa* rescue of 1876, when six Irish Fenian convicts became so desperate to leave Rockingham that they braved a storm to flee in a rickety dinghy. Their motivation is entirely understandable to anyone who has been to Rockingham.

ALSO KNOWN AS Rocko, Rocky, Rockinghole, Cockingham, Crackingham.
MOST FAMOUS PERSON 'Actor' Sam Worthington, otherwise known as Shit Chris Pratt.

AUSTRALIA'S WORST PLACE NAMES

1. Bald Knob, QLD
2. Big Dick Bore, WA
3. Big Knob Waterhole, NT
4. Bonar Street, NSW, VIC & QLD
5. Boobs Flat, TAS
6. Booby Island, QLD
7. Boomers Bottom, TAS
8. Bottom Hole, TAS
9. Break Wind Reserve, SA
10. Bullshit Hill, SA
11. Bum Bum Creek, QLD
12. Burnt Pussy Mine, SA
13. Chinaman's Knob, NSW & VIC
14. Cock Wash, SA
15. Dancing Dicks Creek, NSW
16. Dead Womans Hole, NSW
17. Diapur, VIC
18. Dirty Dick Creek, QLD
19. Double Knob, QLD
20. Finger Buttress, VIC
21. Funny Knob Creek, TAS
22. Goat Knob, NSW
23. Grey Dick Hill, NSW
24. Groper Grotto, SA
25. Guys Dirty Hole, TAS
26. Hooker Park, NSW
27. Hopping Dicks Creek, NSW
28. Horny Point, SA

Honourable mention.

29. Horse Knob, NSW
30. Innaloo, WA
31. Intercourse Island, WA
32. Licking Hole, NSW
33. Lovely Bottom, TAS
34. Minger Well, WA
35. Mossy Nipple Bend, TAS
36. Mount Breast, QLD
37. Mount Buggery, SA
38. Peculiar Nob, SA
39. Pensioners Bush, TAS
40. Pisspot Creek, TAS
41. Prickly Bottom, TAS
42. Shaving Holes Creek, NSW
43. Soily Bottom Point, NSW
44. Stinkhole, TAS
45. The Butts, TAS
46. The Nipples, TAS
47. Tittybong, VIC
48. Titwobble Lane, VIC
49. Wanka Road, QLD
50. Wanky Creek, NSW

INDEX

Bold entries indicate images.

The entrance sign at Goodna, Queensland.

IMAGE CREDITS

FRONT COVER AND P. 135 Zeytun Images/Dreamstime.com; **BACK COVER** Daniele Nabissi/Unsplash; **P. 2** David Downie; **P. 8 (TOP LEFT AND BOTTOM RIGHT)** Alizada Studios/Shutterstock.com; **P. 8 (TOP RIGHT)** Alex Cimbal/Shutterstock.com; **P. 8 (BOTTOM LEFT**) Fosnez/Wikimedia Commons; **P. 14** Wikimedia Commons; **P. 16** Alex Cimbal/Shutterstock.com; **P. 18** Jackson Stock Photography/Shutterstock.com; **P. 20** Joshua Ryan/Wikimedia Commons; **P. 21** Vicki Nunn/Pixabay; **P. 23** Kevin Phillips/Pixabay; **P. 25 (LEFT AND RIGHT)** Alizada Studios/Shutterstock.com; **P. 27** Wikimedia Commons; **P. 37** Steve Todd/Shutterstock.com; **P. 39** Linda72/Pixabay; **P. 40** Alex Cimbal/Shutterstock.com; **P. 51** katacarix/Shutterstock.com; **P. 59** Ayush Jain/Unsplash; **P. 61** Matt Endacott/Wikimedia Commons; **P. 63** Janelle Lugge/Shutterstock.com; **P. 68** meh/Pixabay; **P. 72** rcbutcher/Wikimedia Commons; **P. 73** Eduardo Filgueiras/Unsplash; **P. 75** Nicki Mannix/Flickr; **P. 77** Prescott Horn/Unsplash; **P. 79** Nicki Mannix/Flickr; **P. 80** Greg Brave/Shutterstock.com; **P. 83** katacarix/Shutterstock.com; **P. 84** Sarawut Konganantdech/Shutterstock.com; **P. 88** Brayden J/Wikimedia Commons; **P. 90** Sarawut Konganantdech/Shutterstock.com; **P. 96** AnaBee Images/Shutterstock.com; **PP. 98 AND 101** Dorothy Chiron/Shutterstock.com; **P. 108** Michael Baragwanath/Pixabay; **P. 110** Jason Patrick Ross/Shutterstock.com; **P. 113** Babil Kulesi/Pixabay; **P. 114** demamiel62/Shutterstock.com; **PP. 118, 120 AND 123** Gary Houston/Wikimedia Commons; **P. 125** Danae Callister/Unsplash; **P. 126** Norman Allchin/Shutterstock.com; **P. 130** Jason Patrick Ross/Shutterstock.com; **P. 132** Nils Versemann/Shutterstock.com; **P. 142** Ian Crocker/Shutterstock.com; **P. 146** Charles G/Unsplash; **P. 151** Stefan Schüler/Pixabay; **P. 157** Alizada Studios/Shutterstock.com; **P. 158** ennerodesign/Shutterstock.com; **P. 163** Guscoan/Shutterstock.com; **P. 165** fritz16/Shutterstock.com; **P. 169** Rebecca Lintz/Pixabay; **P. 171** B-E/Shutterstock.com; **P. 175** Morphius Film/Shutterstock.com.

First published in 2021

Allen & Unwin
83 Alexander Street
Crows Nest NSW 2065
Australia
Phone: (61 2) 8425 0100
Email: info@allenandunwin.com
Web: www.allenandunwin.com

A catalogue record for this book is available from the National Library of Australia

ISBN 978 1 98854 776 3

Set in 10.5/14pt Sofia Pro Light by Kate Barraclough
Maps by Kate Barraclough
Images as credited on page 175
Printed in China by C & C Offset Printing Co., Ltd

10 9 8 7 6 5 4 3 2 1